Culturally Responsive
Lessons & Activities

Grade 3

Writing: Julie Strohkorb
Content Editing: Lisa Vitarisi Mathews
Teera Robinson
Copy Editing: Cathy Harber
Art Direction: Yuki Meyer
Cover Design: Yuki Meyer
Illustration: Bryan Langdo
Design/Production: Paula Acojido
Yuki Meyer
Jessica Onken

Visit
teaching-standards.com
to view a correlation
of this book.
This is a free service.

**Correlated to
Current Standards**

**Congratulations on your purchase of some of the
finest teaching materials in the world.**

*Photocopying the pages in this book
is permitted for single-classroom use only.
Making photocopies for additional classes
or schools is prohibited.*

For information about other Evan-Moor products, call 1-800-777-4362,
fax 1-800-777-4332, or visit our website, www.evan-moor.com.
Entire contents © 2022 Evan-Moor Corporation
18 Lower Ragsdale Drive, Monterey, CA 93940-5746. Printed in USA.

CPSIA: Bradford & Bigelow, Newburyport, MA USA [12/2022]

Contents

8 Nonfiction, Informational Fiction, and Realistic Fiction Units

The units in this book are about people from diverse backgrounds with different abilities, ethnicities, and origins. Four units feature nonfiction biographical stories or informational fiction stories about people who are inspirational and perseverant. Four units feature realistic fiction stories about authentic situations and challenges that real people experience. Each unit has a different theme and begins with a teacher page that introduces the subject and activities. The story pages and activities are reproducible for students. The unit's theme is shown at the top of each student page.

Examples of themes include:

Believe in Yourself

We Can Learn to Do Things Differently

You Can Learn from Mistakes

Story

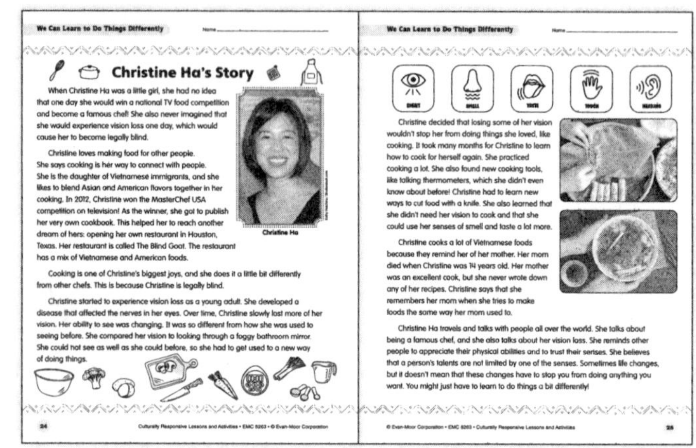

Each of the nonfiction, informational fiction, and realistic fiction units has a reproducible two-page story that the subsequent activities relate to. The story emphasizes the unit's theme.

The stories describe real-life experiences in an age-appropriate way. They tell how people overcame challenges, navigated through complicated situations, and made choices that defined their lives. All of these story subjects and themes were chosen thoughtfully because of their power to inspire and the importance of representation.

Theme-Based Activities

Each unit has an activity that students complete independently, a whole-class or small-group discussion activity, a partner activity, and a project menu. Students choose from hands-on projects, performance projects, and creative writing projects.

Activities in all units vary and are designed to be engaging and open-ended, with a wide variety of response formats. The goal is for students to feel like the activities are providing a "safe space" to share their own unique viewpoints and experiences.

Activities include the following:

- creative writing and drawing
- critical thinking
- visual information
- discussion
- hypothetical scenarios and problem solving
- making choices and justifying opinions
- art projects

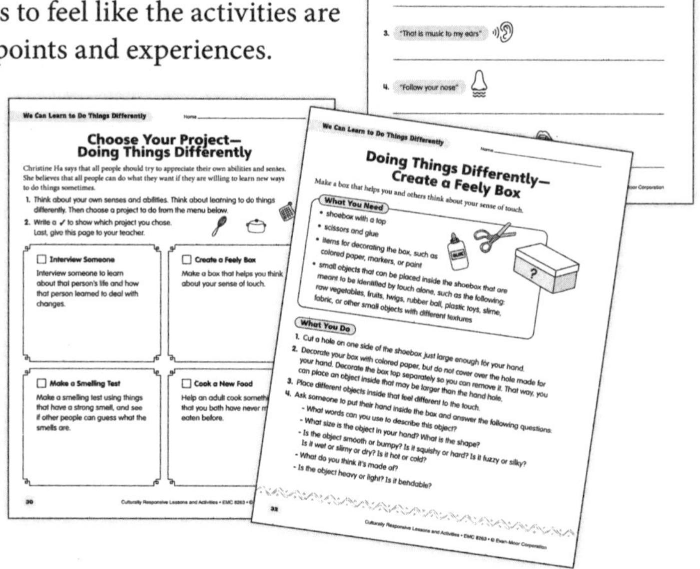

3 Cultural Exploration and Self-Discovery Units

The cultural exploration and self-discovery units are not centered around a text, rather they feature a variety of engaging and creative activities that invite students to reflect on their own cultures and interactions with the world. The activities prompt students to share about their own opinions, tastes, families, and experiences. These activities also support students in being culturally responsive by keeping an open mind, learning about the people around them with the intention of recognizing their value, and considering other viewpoints. Many of the activities provide opportunities for collaboration and whole-class projects. Some collaborative activities include making a class book, comparing handprints, and interviewing their classmates.

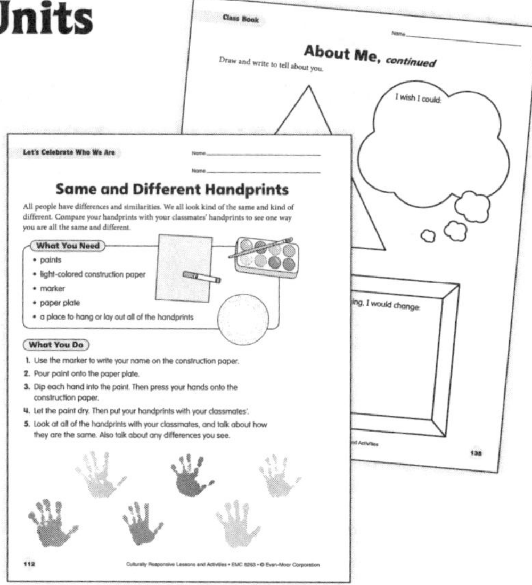

Student Resources

Additional pages provide students with support as well as opportunities for students to take an active role in their learning.

Student Contents

You may wish to allow your students to choose a unit to complete. Reproduce and distribute the Student Contents to students. Review the Student Contents with students. Read aloud the choices of units and descriptions. Have students think about what they are interested in reading, and let the class choose a unit.

How Do I Say It?

Reproduce and distribute the page to students. The text at the top of the page explains the purpose. This page models respectful language that students may choose to use during a class or group discussion. Read aloud the text and sentences on the page as students follow along silently. Discuss with students what listening, showing respect, and being kind looks and sounds like. You may wish to distribute this page to students before you begin the first unit.

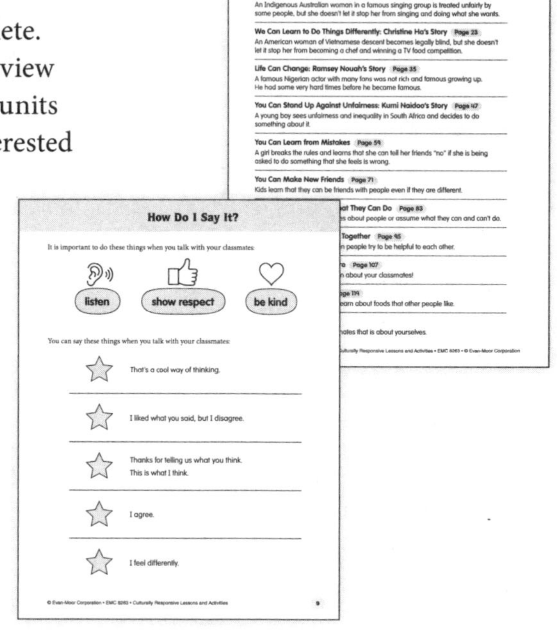

Student and Parent/Guardian Sharing Forms

The Student and Parent/Guardian Sharing Forms are intended to provide a connection between home and school. The purpose is to invite students and their families to communicate directly with the teacher and to take an active role in their learning.

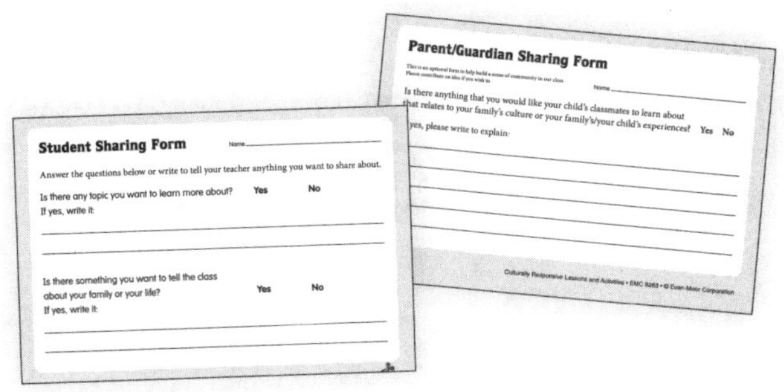

Planning Instruction

Nonfiction, Informational Fiction, and Realistic Fiction Units

Teacher Pages

Each unit begins with a teacher page that summarizes the focus of the unit and provides a suggested teaching path.

Nonfiction, Informational Fiction, and Realistic Fiction Stories

These units center around the story and theme, such as Believe in Yourself. The story provides context for the activities and projects. You can choose the activities that align with your students' needs or provide opportunities to increase engagement and positive interactions among students. Or you can allow students to choose the theme or person they would like to read about by reproducing the Student Contents on page 8 and distributing it to students.

> ## You Can Make New Friends
>
> ### We Can All Be Friends
>
> This unit is about making new friends and giving people a chance. It is also about how to connect friends you already have with the new friends you make. As you guide students through these topics, consider their varying world views as they share their experiences and make connections to their own lives.
>
> The pages in this unit are reproducible. Reproduce the unit in its entirety or choose the pages that you wish to have your students do. A suggested teaching path is below.
>
> 1. **Read the text (pages 72 and 73)**
>   Distribute one copy of the text to each student. Have students read the text independently, or read the text aloud as they follow along silently.
>
> 2. **New Friends! (page 74)**
>   Distribute one copy of the page to each student. Guide students in completing the page independently.
>
> 3. **Let's Talk About the Story (page 75)**
>   Distribute one copy of the page to each student. Facilitate a whole-group discussion or divide the class into small groups.
>
>   **Prepare for discussion:**
>   Tell students that they will have a conversation with classmates about the questions they have been given. Explain that they do not have to write complete answers to the questions. They can write notes about how they want to answer the questions or how they want to respond to other students' comments. Remind students that they can disagree with or add on to what other students say, as long as all students are respectful.
>
> 4. **Talk with Your Partner (pages 76 and 77)**
>   Divide students into groups of two. Distribute one copy of each page to each group. Have each group work on the activity together.
>
> 5. **Choose Your Project—Making Friends (pages 78–82)**
>   Distribute one copy of the project menu to each student. Explain to students that they will each choose a project to do. After students have chosen their project, collect the project menus.
>
>   Reproduce and distribute one of the following project pages to each student based on the student's choice: Page 79 for the card; Page 80 for the video; Page 81 for the list; Page 82 for the poem. Decide whether or not students will share their finished projects with the class and instruct students accordingly.
>
> © Evan-Moor Corporation • EMC 8263 • Culturally Responsive Lessons and Activities 71

Independent Activities

Each nonfiction, informational fiction, and realistic fiction story is followed by an independent activity that provides students opportunities to reflect on the story and the theme and relate it to their own lives.

Discussion Activities

Each unit includes a discussion activity. Before the discussion, students read the discussion items that are based on the story and theme. They are asked to think about their own opinions and experiences, and they may choose to write about them in preparation for the discussion. Before you begin the whole- and small-group discussions, you may wish to reproduce and distribute page 9, How Do I Say It? This page provides ideas and suggestions for statements and sentence starters that encourage respectful and productive communication.

Partner Activities

Each unit includes partner activities that are intended to help students learn about each other as they also learn more about themselves. To prepare for these activities, consider how you will assign partners or what process you will use to have students choose partners. It is important that students connect with classmates that they may not have in their social circle.

Choose Your Project Activities

Each unit includes a project menu for students to choose from. The project choices include hands-on, performance, and creative writing projects. Many of the projects require materials that are commonly part of classroom art supplies. Before you distribute the Choose Your Project activities to students, you may wish to confirm that you have access to the materials needed.

Cultural Exploration and Self-Discovery Units

Teacher Pages

Each unit begins with a teacher page that summarizes the focus of the unit and provides an overview of the activities and projects in the unit.

Activities, Games, and Projects

These units focus on learning about oneself and others through the lens of culture, family traditions, and people's similarities and differences. The activities, games, and projects range from individual to collaborative and often extend to home and family.

The pages in these units do not have to be completed in sequential order. Choose the activities that you want your students to complete, or offer them the opportunity to choose based on their interests.

About Culturally Responsive Teaching and Learning

Culturally responsive teaching is about connecting students' cultures and life experiences with what they are learning in school. Cultural responsiveness is creating a climate in which all students can feel a sense of belonging while also feeling safe to be their authentic selves as they process the curriculum and academic content.

These are some things you might see in a culturally responsive learning environment:

- Student-choice learning activities

- Students sharing about their home lives, first languages, or other cultural and personal experiences

- A sense of community as an emphasis during learning, in addition to academic content

- Family involvement in the learning process

Evan-Moor's Approach to Culturally Responsive Teaching and Learning

The activities in this book are designed to provide students with choices for how to demonstrate their learning and unique viewpoints. Many of the activities, including the group discussions, give students the opportunity to share about their own families and experiences. Our goal is to help students explore their own individualities, cultures, and life experiences and to help them learn more about their classmates, as well as to help teachers gain insights about who their students are so they can make every student's learning more meaningful. The authentic stories in this book represent people from many backgrounds and reflect the diversity and life experiences of people in our world. We hope these stories are both inspiring and enlightening for students.

Student Contents

Believe in Yourself: Laurel Robinson's Story

An Indigenous Australian woman in a famous singing group is treated unfairly by some people, but she doesn't let it stop her from singing and doing what she wants.

We Can Learn to Do Things Differently: Christine Ha's Story

An American woman of Vietnamese descent becomes legally blind, but she doesn't let it stop her from becoming a chef and winning a TV food competition.

Life Can Change: Ramsey Nouah's Story

A famous Nigerian actor with many fans was not rich and famous growing up. He had some very hard times before he became famous.

You Can Stand Up Against Unfairness: Kumi Naidoo's Story

A young boy sees unfairness and inequality in South Africa and decides to do something about it.

You Can Learn from Mistakes

A girl breaks the rules and learns that she can tell her friends "no" if she is being asked to do something that she feels is wrong.

You Can Make New Friends

Kids learn that they can be friends with people even if they are different.

Let Other People Show What They Can Do

Kids learn to not make guesses about people or assume what they can and can't do.

It's Better When We Work Together

Great things can happen when people try to be helpful to each other.

Let's Celebrate Who We Are

Share about yourself and learn about your classmates!

Food Is Part of Culture

Tell about foods you like and learn about foods that other people like.

Class Book

Make a book with your classmates that is about yourselves.

How Do I Say It?

It is important to do these things when you talk with your classmates:

You can say these things when you talk with your classmates:

 That's a cool way of thinking.

 I liked what you said, but I disagree.

 Thanks for telling us what you think.
This is what I think.

 I agree.

 I feel differently.

Student Sharing Form

Name ________________________

Answer the questions below or write to tell your teacher anything you want to share about.

Is there any topic you want to learn more about?   **Yes**   **No**

If yes, write it:

____

____

Is there something you want to tell the class
about your family or your life?   **Yes**   **No**

If yes, write it:

____

____

Parent/Guardian Sharing Form

This is an optional form to help build a sense of community in our class.
Please contribute an idea if you wish to.   Name ________________________

Is there anything that you would like your child's classmates to learn about
that relates to your family's culture or your family's/your child's experiences?   **Yes**   **No**

If yes, please write to explain:

____

____

____

____

Believe in Yourself

Laurel Robinson's Story

This unit is about doing what you love and following your passion, even when other people try to stop you or hold you back. This unit will also show how believing in yourself can help you do kind things for others. Students will read about Laurel Robinson, an Indigenous Australian woman who sang in the music group called The Sapphires and performed for U.S. troops in Vietnam. Students may already know a little about challenges that Indigenous Australians faced in the past, or they may learn about it in this unit. As you guide students through these topics, consider their varying world views as they share their experiences and make connections to their own lives.

The pages in this unit are reproducible. Reproduce the unit in its entirety or choose the pages that you wish to have your students do. A suggested teaching path is below.

1. **Read the Nonfiction Story (pages 12 and 13)**
   Distribute one copy of the text to each student. Have students read the text independently, or read the text aloud as they follow along silently.

2. **I Believe in Myself (page 14)**
   Distribute one copy of the page to each student. Guide students in completing the page independently.

3. **Let's Talk About Laurel Robinson (page 15)**
   Distribute one copy of the page to each student. Facilitate a whole-group discussion or divide the class into small groups.

   Prepare for discussion:
   Tell students that they will have a conversation with classmates about the questions they have been given. Explain that they do not have to write complete answers to the questions. They can write notes about how they want to answer the questions or how they want to respond to other students' comments. Remind students that they can disagree with or add on to what other students say, as long as all students are respectful.

4. **Talk with Your Partner and Believe in Yourself Partner Activity (pages 16 and 17)**
   Divide students into groups of two. Distribute one copy of each page to each group. Have each group work on the activities together.

5. **Choose Your Project—You Can Do Anything (pages 18–22)**
   Distribute one copy of the project menu to each student. Explain to students that they will each choose a project to do. After students have chosen their project, collect the project menus.

   Reproduce and distribute one of the following project pages to each student based on the student's choice: Page 19 for the poster; Page 20 for the sock character; Page 21 for the dance; Page 22 for the song. Decide whether or not students will share their finished projects with the class and instruct students accordingly.

Laurel Robinson's Story

In 1968, four young Indigenous Australian girls believed in themselves. They loved to sing and dance for people. They wanted to sing and dance as a job. Laurel Robinson was one of those girls.

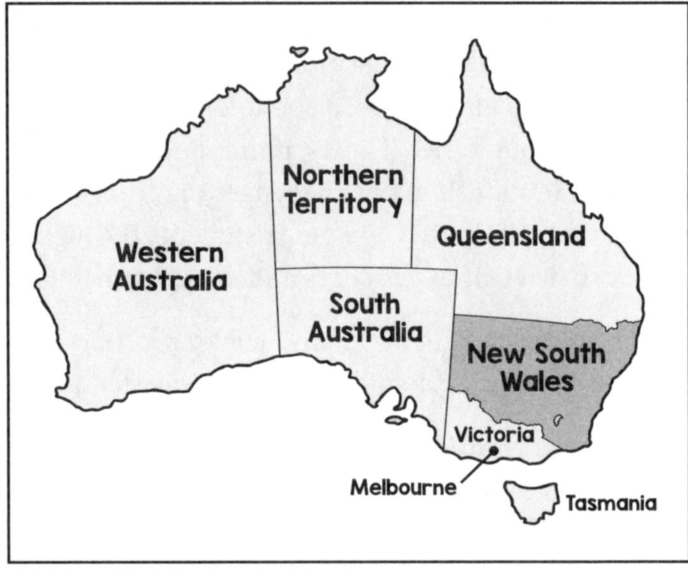

Laurel was part of a proud Yorta Yorta family, a group of Indigenous Australians. They lived in Cummeragunja, Australia, on a reserve, or a reservation. Life was not easy for Indigenous Australians. Reserves did not always have comfortable homes. Sometimes the people living there were not paid well for their work. They did not have enough food for their families. Indigenous Australians were not treated the same as other people in Australia. They knew this was because of their culture and the color of their skin. Laurel knew that this was not fair.

Even though Laurel's family lived a hard life, Laurel, her sister, and her cousins found fun things to do together. They loved to sing and dance for their large family. Their shows made everyone happy. Laurel's grandmother sewed the girls' costumes. Laurel's father glued pennies to the bottom of their shoes so they would make a sound when the girls did tap dancing. As the girls got better and better, they started doing concerts at nearby reserves. They raised money to help the people on their reserve.

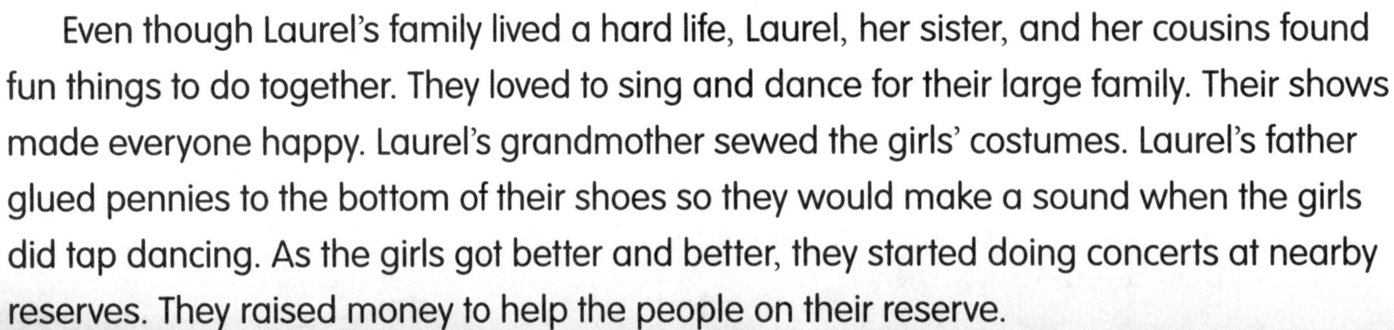

When Laurel was older, she moved to Melbourne, Australia, with her cousins. Laurel looked for work in Melbourne. She saw help wanted signs in the windows and went in to apply for jobs. The shop owners took one look at her and said "no." Laurel knew that this kind of treatment was called racism. Her family and other Indigenous Australians had been treated this way for years. Laurel did not give up. She believed in herself, and she knew she had to work to take care of herself. Laurel and her cousins tried out to sing at a club near their home. They sang the soul music they heard other people of color singing on the radio.

The man who ran the club loved their act and hired them. The girls called their group The Sapphires. They named themselves after the blue gemstone.

Laurel's sister, Lois, also joined the group. The Sapphires performed at different clubs around Australia. It wasn't always easy to find jobs, though. Sometimes they showed up and the club owner would turn them away. But The Sapphires never stopped believing in themselves. They knew they had to keep trying.

Laurel Robinson, Lois Peeler, Beverly Briggs, Naomi Mayers at *The Sapphires* movie premier

One day, someone asked The Sapphires if they would sing for the American troops in Vietnam, where there was a war. Laurel and her sister decided to go. It was frightening to go to a country where there was war. It could be dangerous. But they did it, and the troops loved their act.

The Sapphires were the first popular all-female Indigenous Australian singing group. Laurel Robinson believed she had talent, and she wanted to sing. She, her cousins, and her sister made their dream come true. In 2012, Laurel's son made a movie about The Sapphires. It was the most popular movie in Australia that year.

Name _______________________

I Believe in Myself

Laurel Robinson is an Indigenous Australian who believed in herself, even when other people treated her unfairly. She knew she was a good singer, and she was proud of her family and where she came from. Write inside the shapes to tell 4 reasons why you believe in yourself.

   Culturally Responsive Lessons and Activities • EMC 8263 • © Evan-Moor Corporation

Name _______________________

Let's Talk About Laurel Robinson

Read the questions. Think carefully about how to answer each one.
You will talk with classmates about your ideas. There are no wrong answers.
Below each question, you can write:

Things that you want to say		Things other people said that you agree with		Things other people said that you disagree with

1. What do you think it means for people to "believe in themselves"?

2. Why do you think some people treat other people unfairly?

3. Some people did not give Laurel Robinson a chance because she was from a different culture and she was a person of color. Do you think everyone should be given a chance?

Name

Name

Talk with Your Partner

Laurel Robinson believed in herself, even when other people would not give her a chance. You can believe in yourself about many things. Talk with your partner about what makes you believe in yourselves.

What do you believe in yourselves about?

Being a good reader?

Playing a sport well?

A problem that you can solve?

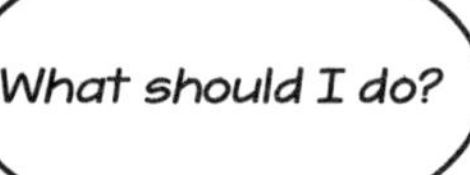

What you will be when you grow up?

Write or draw your own ideas in the box.

Culturally Responsive Lessons and Activities • EMC 8263 • © Evan-Moor Corporation

Name _______________________

Name _______________________

Believe in Yourself Partner Activity

It is not always easy to believe in yourself. Sometimes things can stop you. This activity can help you think about what to do to keep believing in yourself.

1. Cut out the signs below. Each partner will have one **STOP** sign and one **You Can Do It!** sign.

2. On the back of the **STOP** sign, draw or write one thing that may stop you from believing in yourself. After you finish, give the **STOP** sign to your partner.

3. Look at the **STOP** sign your partner gave you. Write or draw something on the back of the **You Can Do It!** sign to help your partner believe in himself or herself. Then give the **You Can Do It!** sign to your partner.

Name ________________________

Choose Your Project— You Can Do Anything

Laurel Robinson is an Indigenous Australian. She and her family were sometimes treated unfairly. But Laurel was very proud of her indigenous background, and she believed in herself. She felt like she could do what she wanted, and she did!

1. Think about the things you want to do in your life. Then choose a project to do from the menu below.

2. Write a ✓ to show which project you chose. Then give this page to your teacher.

☐ **Make a Poster**

Make a poster that you can hang up to help you remember to believe in yourself.

☐ **Make a Cuddly Sock Character**

Make a sock character that you can cuddle with and that can help comfort you when things get tough.

☐ **Do a Dance**

Record a video of yourself doing a dance to music that makes you feel happy and feel like moving.

☐ **Sing a Song**

Record yourself singing a song that you love and that makes you feel good.

Name ________________________

You Can Do Anything—Poster

Make a poster to pump up your energy and to remind yourself that you can do anything.

What You Need

- large sheet of colored construction paper
- markers or crayons
- materials to decorate the poster, such as scissors, dried noodles, glue, colored tissue paper, glitter, stickers, magazine cutouts, paint, and other available materials

What You Do

1. Write a message to encourage yourself on the poster.
2. Decorate the poster.
3. Hang your poster in your room.

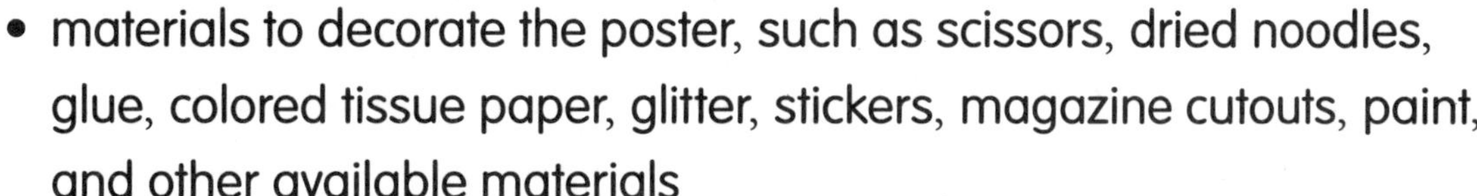

Plan Your Poster

Name _______________________

You Can Do Anything—Sock Character

Make a soft and cuddly sock character to comfort you and help you when times are tough.

What You Need

- fluffy sock
- any soft fabric or cotton balls
- yarn
- materials to make a face and hair on the character, such as beads, buttons, glue, colored duct tape, dried pasta, glitter, more yarn, markers, paint, pompoms, etc.

What You Do

1. Stuff the sock with the soft fabric and/or cotton balls until it is full.
2. Tie the open end of the sock with yarn so it stays closed.
3. Decorate the sock with a face and hair if you'd like.
4. Keep your sock character somewhere handy!

Plan Your Sock Character

Name _______________________

You Can Do Anything—Dance

Record a dance video to help get your energy pumping!

What You Need

- smartphone or other device that can record a video
- music to play and dance to
- an outfit or any props to use in your dance, such as a flag or a hat

What You Do

1. Find a song to dance to.

2. Gather any props or put on any special clothing items you want to wear in your dance.

3. If you want to, use the box below to plan your dance steps or moves before you do it. Or you can just dance from your heart and make up the moves as you go!

4. Record yourself dancing to the music or ask someone to help you record the video.

5. Watch the video to make sure you like it. You can record it again if you want to try again.

6. Show your video to other people.

Plan Your Dance

Name _______________________________

You Can Do Anything—Song

Record yourself singing a song that makes you feel good.

What You Need

- smartphone or other device that can record a video
- an outfit or any props to use as you sing
- a song to sing

What You Do

1. Find a song that you want to sing. Find the words to the song. Write them or print them out.

2. Use a smartphone or other device to record a video or just the sound of you singing the song. If you choose to make a video, you can use props or wear a special outfit if you'd like.

3. Watch or listen to the recording. You can record it again if you want to.

4. When your recording is finished, show it to someone.

Plan Your Song

We Can Learn to Do Things Differently

Christine Ha's Story

This unit is about learning to adapt to new and different abilities in life. Sometimes our abilities change, and we must figure out new ways to do things. Students will read about Christine Ha, a famous chef who is legally blind. While not all students can identify with experiencing a disability, Christine Ha's story shows how a positive attitude and perseverance can help people to try their best and to try new things. As you guide students through these topics, consider their varying world views as they share their experiences and make connections to their own lives.

The pages in this unit are reproducible. Reproduce the unit in its entirety or choose the pages that you wish to have your students do. A suggested teaching path is below.

1. **Read the Nonfiction Story (pages 24 and 25)**

   Distribute one copy of the text to each student. Have students read the text independently, or read the text aloud as they follow along silently.

2. **Changes Can Strengthen You (page 26)**

   Distribute one copy of the page to each student. Guide students in completing the page independently.

3. **Let's Talk About Christine Ha (page 27)**

   Distribute one copy of the page to each student. Facilitate a whole-group discussion or divide the class into small groups.

   Prepare for discussion:

   Tell students that they will have a conversation with classmates about the questions they have been given. Explain that they do not have to write complete answers to the questions. They can write notes about how they want to answer the questions or how they want to respond to other students' comments. Remind students that they can disagree with or add on to what other students say, as long as all students are respectful.

4. **Talk with Your Partner and Partner Challenge (pages 28 and 29)**

   Divide students into groups of two. Distribute one copy of each page to each group. Have each group work on the activities together.

5. **Choose Your Project—Doing Things Differently (pages 30–34)**

   Distribute one copy of the project menu to each student. Explain to students that they will each choose a project to do. After students have chosen their project, collect the project menus.

   Reproduce and distribute one of the following project pages to each student based on the student's choice: Page 31 for the interview; Page 32 for the feely box; Page 33 for the smelling test; Page 34 for the new food. Decide whether or not students will share their finished projects with the class and instruct students accordingly.

Name _______________________________________

Christine Ha's Story

When Christine Ha was a little girl, she had no idea that one day she would win a national TV food competition and become a famous chef! She also never imagined that she would experience vision loss one day, which would cause her to become legally blind.

Christine loves making food for other people. She says cooking is her way to connect with people. She is the daughter of Vietnamese immigrants, and she likes to blend Asian and American flavors together in her cooking. In 2012, Christine won the MasterChef USA competition on television! As the winner, she got to publish her very own cookbook. This helped her to reach another dream of hers: opening her own restaurant in Houston, Texas. Her restaurant is called The Blind Goat. The restaurant has a mix of Vietnamese and American foods.

Christine Ha

Kathy Hutchins / Shutterstock.com

Cooking is one of Christine's biggest joys, and she does it a little bit differently from other chefs. This is because Christine is legally blind.

Christine started to experience vision loss as a young adult. She developed a disease that affected the nerves in her eyes. Over time, Christine slowly lost more of her vision. Her ability to see was changing. It was so different from how she was used to seeing before. She compared her vision to looking through a foggy bathroom mirror. She could not see as well as she could before, so she had to get used to a new way of doing things.

     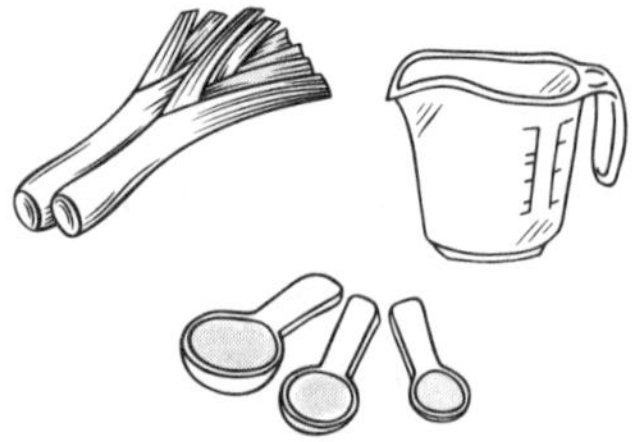

 SIGHT  SMELL  TASTE  TOUCH 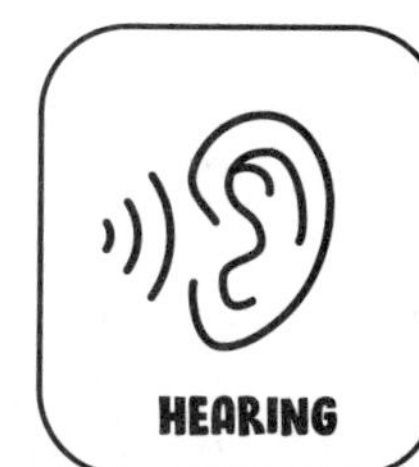 HEARING

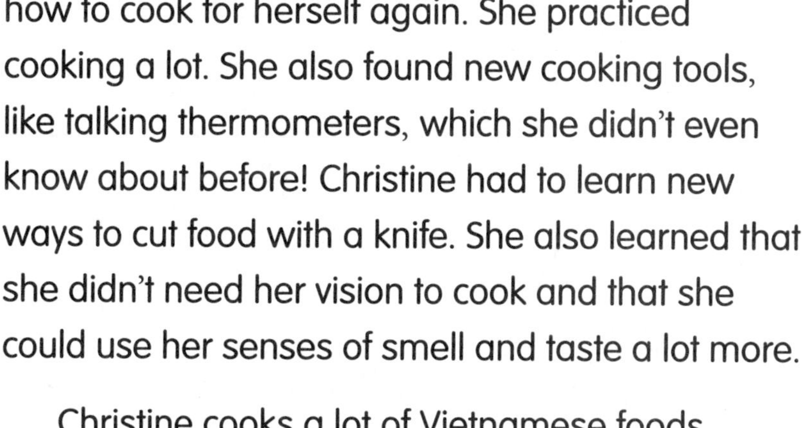

Christine decided that losing some of her vision wouldn't stop her from doing things she loved, like cooking. It took many months for Christine to learn how to cook for herself again. She practiced cooking a lot. She also found new cooking tools, like talking thermometers, which she didn't even know about before! Christine had to learn new ways to cut food with a knife. She also learned that she didn't need her vision to cook and that she could use her senses of smell and taste a lot more.

Christine cooks a lot of Vietnamese foods because they remind her of her mother. Her mom died when Christine was 14 years old. Her mother was an excellent cook, but she never wrote down any of her recipes. Christine says that she remembers her mom when she tries to make foods the same way her mom used to.

Christine Ha travels and talks with people all over the world. She talks about being a famous chef, and she also talks about her vision loss. She reminds other people to appreciate their physical abilities and to trust their senses. She believes that a person's talents are not limited by one of the senses. Sometimes life changes, but it doesn't mean that these changes have to stop you from doing anything you want. You might just have to learn to do things a bit differently!

Name ______________________________

Changes Can Strengthen You

Christine Ha had a big life change when she experienced vision loss as an adult. But she didn't let that stop her from doing the things she liked.

Draw and write a greeting card for someone who is going through a big life change.

Greeting Card Cover

Greeting Card Message

Name ___________________________

Let's Talk About Christine Ha

Read the questions. Think carefully about how to answer each one.
You will talk with classmates about your ideas. There are no wrong answers.
Below each question, you can write:

Things that you want to say	 Things other people said that you agree with	 Things other people said that you disagree with

1. Think of a time when you had to change your plans or something turned out differently from how you thought it would. How did you feel?

2. Do you agree with Christine Ha that people can do whatever they want even if their abilities change? Why or why not?

3. Cooking Vietnamese food helps Christine feel close to her mom. What kinds of things help you feel closer to other people?

4. Do you think it would be hard to learn how to do things in a whole new way like Christine did? Tell why you think yes or no.

Name ________________________

Name ________________________

Talk with Your Partner 

People use their senses every day. Read the idioms below. They are about using your senses. With your partner, try to guess the meanings of the idioms. Then write what you think each idiom really means.

What is an Idiom?

An idiom is a phrase that really means something different from what the words say.

1. "To keep in touch with someone" 

____

2. "To see things eye to eye" 

____

3. "That is music to my ears" 

____

4. "Follow your nose" 

____

5. "To get a taste of your own medicine"  

____

   Culturally Responsive Lessons and Activities • EMC 8263 • © Evan-Moor Corporation

Name ______________________________

Name ______________________________

  # Partner Challenge 

Do these activities with your partner. When you are finished, talk about how hard or easy you found these activities. Think about how you would feel if you had to learn to do things differently every day.

1. Learning to Do Something Differently: Writing

Write a note to your partner using the hand you do not write with every day. Can your partner read the note? Discuss what was hard about trying to write this way.

2. Learning to Do Something Differently: Drawing

Sit back to back with your partner so you cannot see each other. Tell your partner what to draw, step by step. Tell your partner the shapes and sizes to draw. After you're done, look at the picture your partner drew. Does it look like the picture you imagined and were describing?

Name _______________________

Choose Your Project— Doing Things Differently

Christine Ha says that all people should try to appreciate their own abilities and senses. She believes that all people can do what they want if they are willing to learn new ways to do things sometimes.

1. Think about your own senses and abilities. Think about learning to do things differently. Then choose a project to do from the menu below.

2. Write a ✓ to show which project you chose. Last, give this page to your teacher.

☐ **Interview Someone**

Interview someone to learn about that person's life and how that person learned to deal with changes.

☐ **Create a Feely Box**

Make a box that helps you think about your sense of touch.

☐ **Make a Smelling Test**

Make a smelling test using things that have a strong smell, and see if other people can guess what the smells are.

☐ **Cook a New Food**

Help an adult cook something new that you both have never made or eaten before.

Name ________________

Doing Things Differently—Interview

Interview an adult. Use the questions below. Then write a question of your own inside the box for number 5. Write the person's answers on the lines.

1. Did you ever have to make a big change in how you do something in your daily life? If yes, what was it? If not, tell me what would be the hardest thing for you to change about your daily life.

____

____

2. What is one way that you are different now from how you were as a kid?

____

____

3. Do you like to make a lot of changes in your life? Or do you like to keep things the same for a long time? Why?

____

____

4. Do you think that using technology is one way to learn how to do things differently? And do you like learning how to use new kinds of technology?

____

____

5.

____

____

   Name _______________________

Doing Things Differently— Create a Feely Box

Make a box that helps you and others think about your sense of touch.

What You Need

- shoebox with a top
- scissors and glue
- items for decorating the box, such as colored paper, markers, or paint
- small objects that can be placed inside the shoebox that are meant to be identified by touch alone, such as the following: raw vegetables, fruits, twigs, rubber ball, plastic toys, slime, fabric, or other small objects with different textures

What You Do

1. Cut a hole on one side of the shoebox just large enough for your hand.

2. Decorate your box with colored paper, but do not cover over the hole made for your hand. Decorate the box top separately so you can remove it. That way, you can place an object inside that may be larger than the hand hole.

3. Place different objects inside that feel different to the touch.

4. Ask someone to put their hand inside the box and answer the following questions:

    - What words can you use to describe this object?

    - What size is the object in your hand? What is the shape?

    - Is the object smooth or bumpy? Is it squishy or hard? Is it fuzzy or silky? Is it wet or slimy or dry? Is it hot or cold?

    - What do you think it's made of?

    - Is the object heavy or light? Is it bendable?

   Culturally Responsive Lessons and Activities • EMC 8263 • © Evan-Moor Corporation

Name _______________________

Doing Things Differently— Make a Smelling Test

Make a smelling test that helps you and others think about your sense of smell.

What You Need

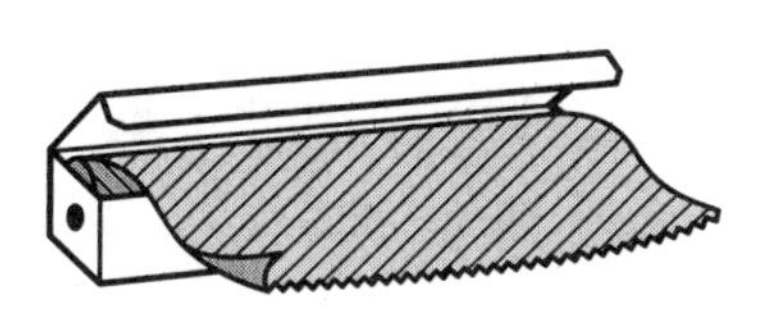

- 3 or more empty, clean containers such as bowls, paper plates, cups, or jars
- aluminum foil
- toothpick or other sharp point
- rubber bands
- items with a strong smell that are safe, such as spices and herbs (like cinnamon, oregano, nutmeg, garlic salt, vanilla, and others), maple syrup, orange peels, onion slices, pickles, coffee, or freshly cut fruit

What You Do

1. Place each smelly item in a different container.
2. Place foil over the container or over the smelly item.
3. Use the toothpick to poke small holes in the top of the foil.
4. Ask someone to do the smelling test. First, that person has to cover his or her eyes. Next, he or she has to smell the items through the holes in the foil. Last, ask the person to guess each item that he or she smelled.

Have Fun!

Name _________________________

Doing Things Differently— Cook a New Food

Christine Ha uses food to connect to her mother and to other people. She had to learn how to make food differently from how she used to cook. You can also make food with someone and try doing something new in the kitchen!

What You Need

- an adult to help you cook
- recipe for a food that you and the adult never had before

What You Do

1. Ask an adult to help you find a recipe that you can both make together. Find a recipe for a food that you both have never made or eaten before.

2. Gather all of the ingredients and things you need to make the recipe.

3. Ask an adult to help you make the recipe.

4. After you have finished making the food, eat it!

Plan Your Recipe

Life Can Change

This unit is about recognizing that everyone faces obstacles in their lives. Even people whom we may consider to be successful have gone through their own challenges and hardships, and that's why it's important not to make the assumption that someone has had an "easy life." Students will read about Ramsey Nouah, a Nigerian actor, who had many hardships during the early part of his life, but he didn't stop dreaming, and his life changed. As you guide students through these topics, consider their varying world views as they share their experiences and make connections to their own lives.

The pages in this unit are reproducible. Reproduce the unit in its entirety or choose the pages that you wish to have your students do. A suggested teaching path is below.

1. **Read the Informational Fiction Story (pages 36 and 37)**
   Distribute one copy of the text to each student. Have students read the text independently, or read the text aloud as they follow along silently.

2. **What Would You Change? (page 38)**
   Distribute one copy of the page to each student. Guide students in completing the page independently.

3. **Let's Talk About Ramsey Nouah (page 39)**
   Distribute one copy of the page to each student. Facilitate a whole-group discussion or divide the class into small groups.

   Prepare for discussion:
   Tell students that they will have a conversation with classmates about the questions they have been given. Explain that they do not have to write complete answers to the questions. They can write notes about how they want to answer the questions or how they want to respond to other students' comments. Remind students that they can disagree with or add on to what other students say, as long as all students are respectful.

4. **Talk with Your Partner and Guess the Job with Your Partner! (pages 40 and 41)**
   Divide students into groups of two. Distribute one copy of page 40 to each student. Distribute one copy of page 41 to each group. Have each group work on the activities together.

5. **Choose Your Project—I Can Help Give Hope (pages 42–46)**
   Distribute one copy of the project menu to each student. Explain to students that they will each choose a project to do. After students have chosen their project, collect the project menus.

   Reproduce and distribute one of the following project pages to each student based on the student's choice: Page 43 for the book; Page 44 for the video message; Page 45 for the picture; Page 46 for the poem. Decide whether or not students will share their finished projects with the class and instruct students accordingly.

Name ___________________

Ramsey Nouah's Story

I couldn't stop thinking about the story Aunt Abishola told me about Ramsey Nouah. He is one of her favorite actors. Ramsey Nouah is from Nigeria, a country in Africa. My aunt told me that Ramsey Nouah had a hard life before he became famous. "When I see him in movies and magazines, I can hardly believe that he did not have enough food to eat or a place to sleep when he was young," she said. "Hakeem, you know that Ramsey is a big movie star, so I just thought he always had an easy life. But his life wasn't always so easy."

"Hmm, I guess people's lives can change," I thought.

Aunt Abishola explained that many families go through some of the same things that Ramsey's did. He only had one parent, his mom. She could not work very much when he was a baby because she had to stay home to take care of him. That meant that Ramsey and his mom did not always have enough money to buy food to eat. It also meant that sometimes they did not have a place to live.

My aunt saw an interview where Ramsey talked about how hard life was for him and his family when he was growing up. He said that he still remembers his stomach rumbling from being hungry when he was a little boy. He also remembers his mom going from shop to shop to ask if any of the shop owners would let them sleep on their floor. He and his mom looked at each other and smiled when one of the shop owners said yes. Even though the mat was thin and the floor was hard and cold, at least they would not have to sleep outside in the rain.

Aunt Abishola had tears in her eyes when she told me his story. I felt sad for him. I have food, and I have a warm bed to sleep in. I even have my own bedroom. And Ramsey had so little. But then Aunt Abishola reminded me, "Hakeem, it is not where you are or what you have, it is who you are inside that matters." I thought about what that meant as Aunt Abishola told me more about Ramsey's life.

As Ramsey grew up, he felt happiest when he was watching movies. He loved American movies and Nigerian movies. Ramsey loved watching the actors onscreen. He decided that he wanted to be a movie star one day. "I wonder if I can do it," he thought to himself often.

Ramsey also liked going to school. As he got older, he still wanted to be an actor. But there were other jobs that Ramsey was thinking of doing, too. He thought about becoming an engineer. He loved planes, machines, and gadgets. But he was most interested in acting, and he didn't give up on that. He decided to go to acting school.

Ramsey finally got his chance to start acting when he was 23 years old. He acted in a TV show that was on almost every day. Because Ramsey was on TV so much, people started to recognize him. He became famous quickly. Then he started getting a lot more acting jobs. Today, he is one of the most famous people in Africa!

Ramsey Nouah

Aunt Abishola and I talked about how a person's life can change. We thought about how Ramsey Nouah and his mom and so many other people go through hard times. We thought about how each of those people will do something different in this world. Not all of them will become famous actors.

"Aunt Abishola, I'm glad Ramsey never lost hope to have a better life. I'm glad he knew that his life could change."

"So am I, Hakeem. Now let's make some popcorn and watch Ramsey in *Merry Men*. That movie is so funny, and I feel like laughing!"

Name _______________________

What Would You Change?

Ramsey Nouah's life changed. When he was young, he had some tough times. But he never lost hope, and things got better. In the circles, write or draw one thing that you would change about your life and one thing that you would not change.

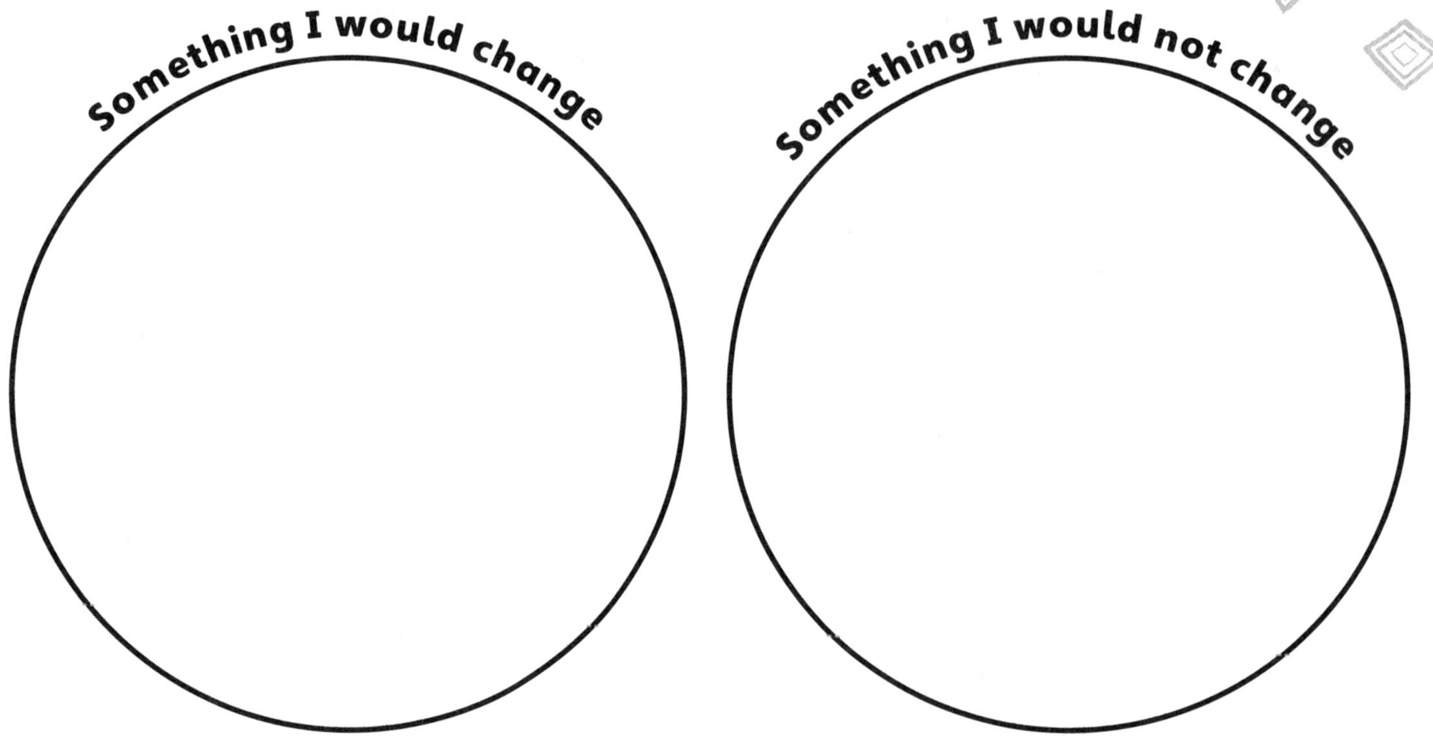

When Ramsey Nouah was young, he felt happy watching movies.
Write or draw yourself doing something that makes you feel happy.

Culturally Responsive Lessons and Activities • EMC 8263 • © Evan-Moor Corporation

Name _______________________

Let's Talk About Ramsey Nouah

Read the questions. Think carefully about how to answer each one.
You will talk with classmates about your ideas. There are no wrong answers.
Below each question, you can write:

| Things that you want to say |  | Things other people said that you agree with |  | Things other people said that you disagree with |

1. All people have hard things that they go through in their lives. Different people have different kinds of hardships. In your opinion, why is it important to remember this?

2. Do you think that anyone can change their life? Tell why you have your opinion.

3. Ramsey Nouah remembers the hard times he went through in the past. Do you think it's good to try to remember hard times in the past so you can learn from them? Or is it better to try to forget hard times?

4. Do you think that going through hard times can make people stronger in the end? Why or why not?

Name ______________________________

Name ______________________________

Talk with Your Partner

One way that life changes is that you can get a job. Ramsey Nouah knew that he wanted to be an actor when he grew up. Do you know what jobs you might want to do when you grow up? Read the list of jobs below. Write a ✓ next to any jobs that you think you might want to do. Then write a reason why. Last, share your answers with your partner.

Career	Reason
Actor	
Athlete	
Chef	
Dancer	
Detective	
Doctor	
Firefighter	
Game designer	
Lawyer	
Musician	
Pilot	
Scientist	
Store manager	
Teacher	
Veterinarian	
Writer	
Other:	

Name _______________________________

Name _______________________________

Guess the Job with Your Partner!

Each card has a job name. Cut out the cards. Then shuffle the cards and place them facedown in a pile. Decide which partner will be Partner 1 and Partner 2. Next, follow the steps below to play the game.

Steps to Play the Game

1. Partner 1 picks up a card and without looking at it, shows it to his or her partner, and puts it facedown.

2. Partner 1 has to guess what job is on the card. Partner 2 gives clues without saying any words on the card. Partner 2 can say words or do actions to give clues.

3. After Partner 1 guesses the job or gives up, it is Partner 2's turn to pick a card and guess the job!

4. Continue playing until time runs out.

Dentist	Parachute jumper	Musician
Nurse	Video game tester	Chef
Clothing designer	Illustrator	Teacher
Bus driver	Gardener	Server in a restaurant

Name ___________________________

Choose Your Project—
I Can Help Give Hope

Ramsey Nouah went through some very hard times in his life. But he always had hope that life could change and that things could get better. You can make something to try to give other people hope when they are going through hard times, too.

1. Think about messages that help you feel hopeful. Then choose a project from the menu below.

2. Write a ✓ to show which project you chose. Then give this page to your teacher.

☐ Create a Book

Create a small book that has messages of hope for someone.

☐ Record a Video Message

Use a smartphone or device to record an inspiring message for someone to have hope.

☐ Make a Picture

Make a picture to help someone feel hopeful.

☐ Write an Acrostic Poem

Use a person's name to write an acrostic poem about all the things you like about that person.

Name _______________________

I Can Help Give Hope—Create a Book

Create a book with hopeful messages and pictures for someone.

What You Need

- 3 sheets of white paper
- stapler
- markers or colored pencils

What You Do

1. Place the 3 sheets of paper on top of each other. Fold them in half like a book. Then staple them together on the left side.

2. Write a title for your book on the front cover. Draw a picture on the cover.

3. On each page inside the book, write a kind or hopeful message. You can write a quote from a poem or a song if you'd like. Then draw pictures inside the book.

4. Give your book to someone or share the book with your friends.

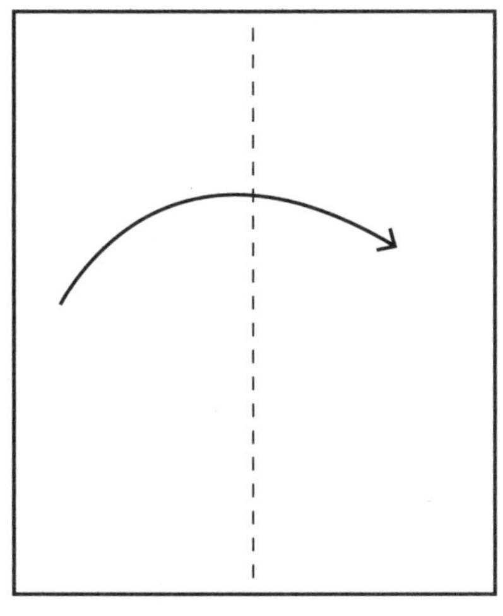

fold them in half

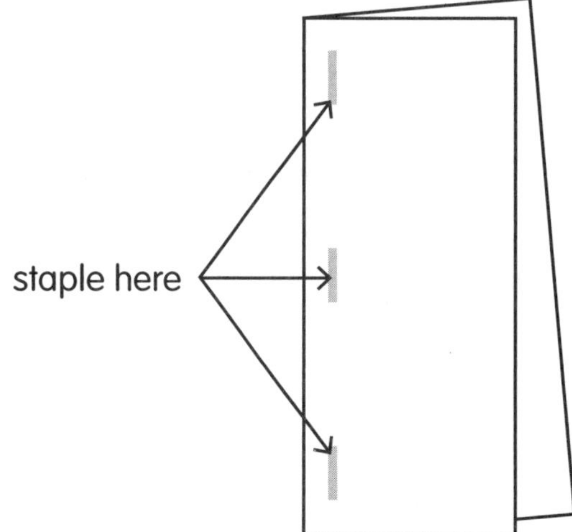

Name _______________________

I Can Help Give Hope— Record a Video Message

Record a short hopeful video message!

What You Need

- smartphone or other device that can record a video
- any objects you want to wear or use in the video, or music
- index card
- pencil

What You Do

1. Write what you want to say in your video message on the index card.
2. Record your video message. You can read from the index card.
3. Share your video with your class.

Plan Your Message

Name _______________________

I Can Help Give Hope—Make a Picture

Make a picture that can help someone feel hopeful.

What You Need

- sheet of light-colored construction paper
- materials to make a picture, such as colored pencils, paint, crayons, glue, glitter, scissors, colored tissue paper, cotton balls, buttons, beads, foil, etc.

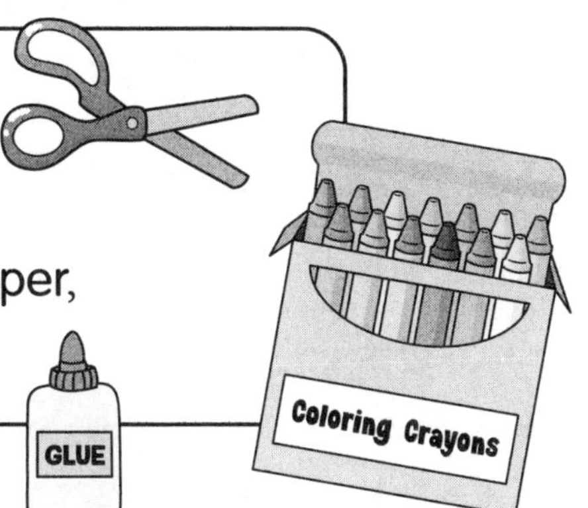

What You Do

1. Make a picture of anything that you think could make someone feel happy or hopeful.

2. Hang up your picture or show your picture to other people.

Plan Your Picture

Name ______________________

I Can Help Give Hope—
Write an Acrostic Poem

Write a poem that tells someone the things you like about that person or the things you like to do with that person.

What You Need

- light-colored construction paper
- markers or crayons

What You Do

1. Write the letters of the person's name from top to bottom on the left side of the paper. Write all capital letters.

2. Write a phrase that begins with each letter of the person's name.

3. Draw pictures on the paper to make it colorful.

4. Give your poem to the person whose name you wrote.

Plan Your Poem

You Can Stand Up Against Unfairness

Kumi Naidoo's Story

This unit is about identifying and addressing injustice in the world. Children of all ages can identify unfairness and can have a strong sense of justice. Students will read about Kumi Naidoo, who as a child living in South Africa, recognized unfairness in the world around him and organized action to stand up against it. With practice, students can learn how to deal with problems respectfully and proactively. As you guide students through these topics, consider their varying world views as they share their experiences and make connections to their own lives.

The pages in this unit are reproducible. Reproduce the unit in its entirety or choose the pages that you wish to have your students do. A suggested teaching path is below.

1. **Read the Nonfiction Story (pages 48 and 49)**

   Distribute one copy of the text to each student. Have students read the text independently, or read the text aloud as they follow along silently.

2. **Have the Courage to Speak Up (page 50)**

   Distribute one copy of the page to each student. Guide students in completing the page independently.

3. **Let's Talk About Kumi Naidoo (page 51)**

   Distribute one copy of the page to each student. Facilitate a whole-group discussion or divide the class into small groups.

   Prepare for discussion:

   Tell students that they will have a conversation with classmates about the questions they have been given. Explain that they do not have to write complete answers to the questions. They can write notes about how they want to answer the questions or how they want to respond to other students' comments. Remind students that they can disagree with or add on to what other students say, as long as all students are respectful.

4. **Talk with Your Partner and What Can You Do About the Problem? (pages 52 and 53)**

   Divide students into groups of two. Distribute one copy of each page to each group. Have each group work on the activities together.

5. **Choose Your Project—Tell About a Problem (pages 54–58)**

   Distribute one copy of the project menu to each student. Explain to students that they will each choose a project to do. After students have chosen their project, collect the project menus.

   Reproduce and distribute one of the following project pages to each student based on the student's choice: Page 55 for the poster; Page 56 for the letter; Page 57 for the donation box; Page 58 for the video. Decide whether or not students will share their finished projects with the class and instruct students accordingly.

Name _______________________

Kumi Naidoo's Story

Kumi pressed his cheek against the city bus window. He was finally twelve years old, so he could take trips into the city without his parents. This was his first bus trip alone. He saw large markets, big houses, and shopping malls whizzing by. It all looked so different from his little village.

As the bus stopped in traffic, Kumi saw a city schoolyard on the corner. It looked much nicer than his school back home. He saw a group of boys his age kicking a red rubber ball into a large net. Kumi and his friends only had oranges to kick, if they could find some. This school had hopscotch games painted on a smooth blacktop and colorful climbing bars. Kumi and his classmates only had trees to climb. Suddenly, Kumi's stomach felt tight. This fancy school was only a short bus ride from his school. How could it be so different? Kumi thought this school was so much better than his.

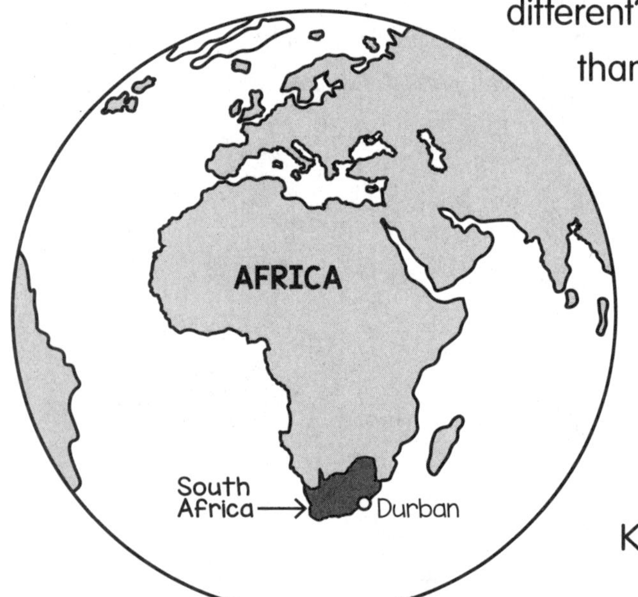

At an early age, Kumi Naidoo saw unfairness in his hometown, near Durban, South Africa. It made him feel angry and jealous. "It's so unfair that some people have so much while others have so little," he thought. He wished he had a fine student uniform like these boys wore in the schoolyard. Kumi decided to do something about it.

Years before Kumi was born, South Africans were used to rules that said that people had to be divided by skin color. People of many races and backgrounds lived in South Africa, but they were forced to live and work separately. Their neighborhoods were kept apart. Their schools were separate. Their stores and seats in public places were always kept apart. People with lighter skin seemed to have better places to live and better schools than people with darker skin. Kumi didn't understand why, but he knew it wasn't fair.

When Kumi was 15 years old, he decided to take a stand against the unfairness. He and many other students marched in the streets to demand better schools for children. They chanted loudly, "Our teachers get paid peanuts!" Many of Kumi's friends got into big trouble for making unrest. Some even went to jail. But Kumi decided that a fair education was too important to stay silent. This was just the first time of many that Kumi took a stand against unfairness.

Today, Kumi is known as an activist. An activist is a person who has the courage to stand up against unfairness. If you tell lots of people about a problem, then more people will know about it and possibly care about it. Then more people will want to stand up against the unfairness. It took many years for Kumi and other activists to persuade South Africans to change their "stay apart" rules. Kumi helped other people understand that all South Africans are important, no matter their skin color, and that all children should have a fair and equal education.

Kumi sees problems and tries to get world leaders to help fix them. He has been standing up against unfairness since he was a young boy.

imageBROKER / Alamy Stock

Name ___________________

Have the Courage to Speak Up

Standing up against unfairness takes courage, or bravery. Kumi Naidoo speaks up and tells lots of people about the problems he sees in the world around him. Think about a problem that you see or know about that affects other people. Write around the circle to finish each sentence. Then draw inside the circle to show what each sentence tells.

One problem I see or know about is

This problem makes people feel

I want to fix this problem because

One person I can tell about this problem is

Name ______________________________

Let's Talk About Kumi Naidoo

Read the questions. Think carefully about how to answer each one.
You will talk with classmates about your ideas. There are no wrong answers.
Below each question, you can write:

| Things that you want to say |  | Things other people said that you agree with |  | Things other people said that you disagree with |

1. Tell about a time when you saw a problem but felt afraid to speak up.

2. Name something that seems unfair to you. Does it seem unfair to others as well, or do others see it differently?

3. Tell about a time when you had courage. Why did you need courage and how did it help you?

4. What does it mean to "think before you act"?

Name _______________________

Name _______________________

Talk with Your Partner

Read each problem below. Then draw an arrow on the scale to show how much you and your partner care about this problem. If you both care different amounts, draw 2 arrows and write your names by your own arrow.

Problem	Scale

Some people don't have enough food, and they feel hungry.

Some schools do not have good textbooks and safe playground equipment, and some schools do.

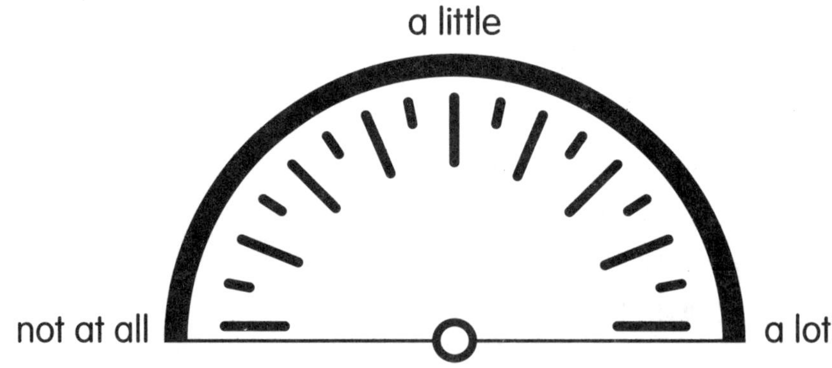

Some people have to leave their country because it's not safe.

What Can You Do About the Problem?

Each card below tells about a different problem. You might be able to solve a problem if you tell someone about it. Cut out the cards and place them in a pile facedown. Take turns with your partner drawing a card. When it's your turn, read the card aloud and tell what you would do if you had that problem.

Problem Card

Every time you try to speak up, your classmate finishes your sentence and interrupts you.

Problem Card

You're afraid to walk down the school hallway because a kid is always waiting there to tease you or trip you.

Problem Card

You are in class and suddenly remember something. You forgot to finish your project, and it's due today!

Problem Card

You want to focus at school, but there is so much noise. The teacher tells you to focus when you get distracted.

Problem Card

You think your classmates don't like you very much. You want to join in their game, but you don't know how.

Problem Card

Your older siblings like to watch stuff on TV that scares you and it makes you have a hard time falling asleep at night.

Problem Card

You have a food allergy. You are not allowed to eat pizza or cupcakes with wheat. But you really want to go to your friend's birthday party.

Problem Card

You feel sad whenever you leave your house or are away from your family.

Name ______________________________________

Choose Your Project—
Tell About a Problem

Kumi Naidoo is an activist. He tries to help the world by telling lots of people about a problem so that lots of people will care and try to help solve it. Anybody can be an activist, even kids.

1. Think about a problem that you know about in your neighborhood or school. Then choose a project to do from the menu below.

2. Write a ✓ to show which project you chose. Then give this page to your teacher.

☐ Make a Poster

Write an important message about a problem on a poster with both words and pictures.

☐ Write a Letter

Write a letter to someone who you think might be able to help with the problem.

☐ Make a Donation Box

Decorate a box to put items in that can be donated to people in need.

☐ Record a Video

Record a video to tell people about a problem.

Name _______________

Tell About a Problem—Make a Poster

Make a poster to tell people about a problem you care about!

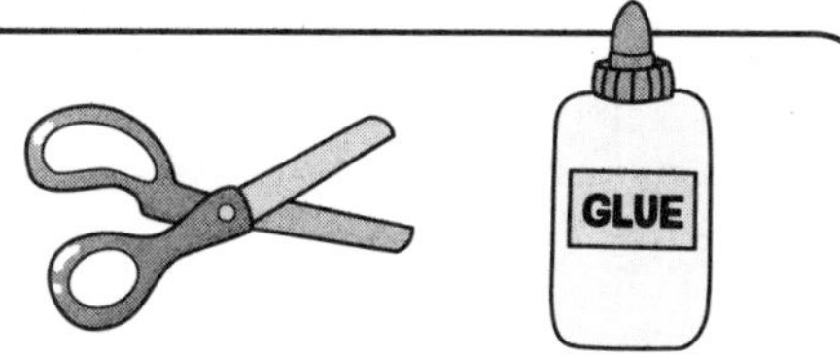

What You Need

- poster board
- markers
- materials to decorate the poster, such as glue, scissors, colored tissue paper, dried pasta, glitter, cotton balls, foil, pompoms, etc.

What You Do

1. Think of the problem you want to tell people about. Think of a message you want to write on your poster, and use the markers to write it.

2. Draw pictures and decorate your poster.

3. Show your poster to your classmates.

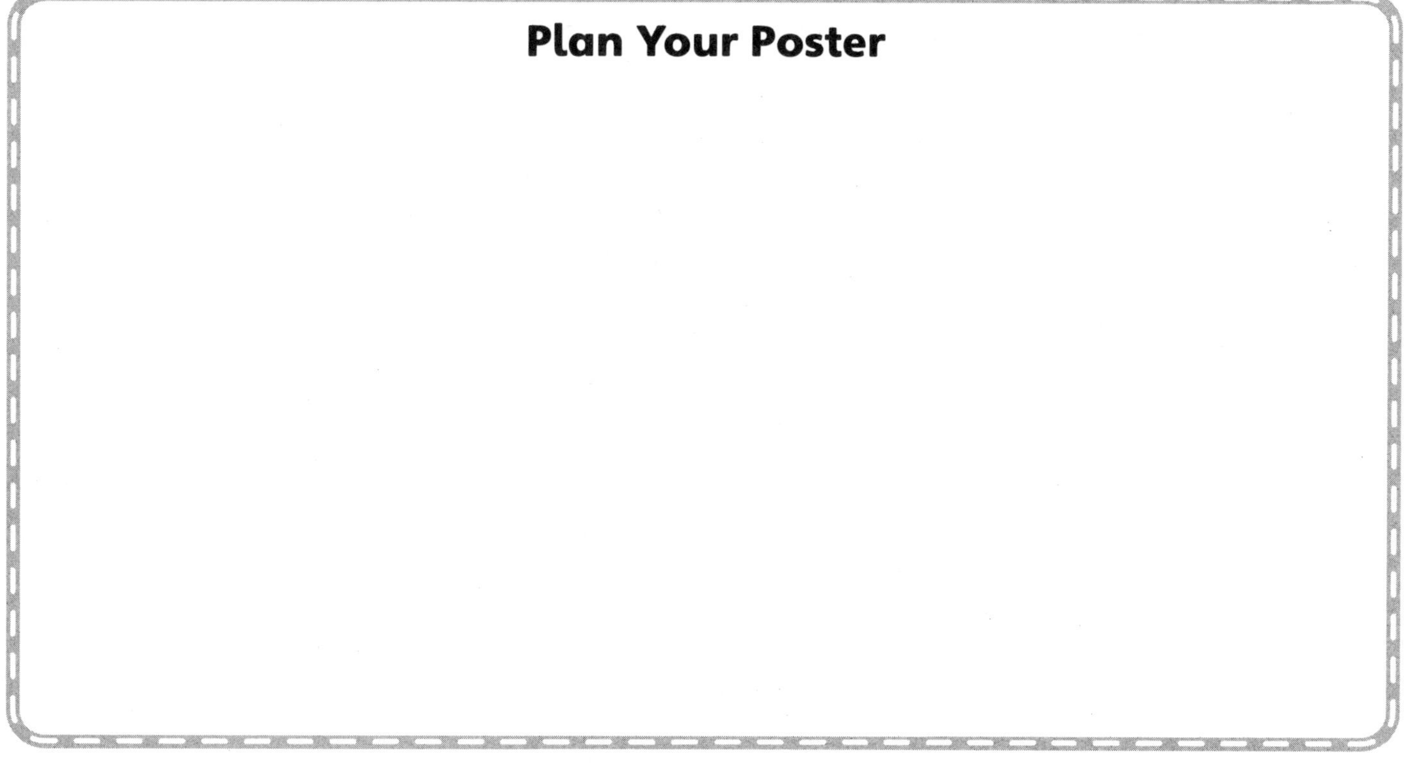

Plan Your Poster

Name _______________________

Tell About a Problem— Write a Letter

Write a letter to tell someone about a problem you care about!

What You Need

- pen
- paper
- envelope

What You Do

1. Think about the problem. Then think about one person who you think might be able to help solve the problem or someone who you want to tell about the problem.

2. Write a letter to the person you chose. Remember to write the date, a greeting, and a closing.

3. Write the person's name on the envelope, and write your name where the return address goes.

4. Show your letter to someone or read it aloud to someone.

Plan Your Letter

Name _______________________________

Tell About a Problem— Make a Donation Box

Make a donation box to put items in that can be donated.

> ## What You Need
>
> - large cardboard box
> - markers
> - materials to decorate the box, such as glue, scissors, colored tissue paper, dried pasta, glitter, cotton balls, foil, pompoms, etc.

What You Do

1. Write the words **Donation Box** on the box using the markers.

2. Use materials to decorate the box.

3. Keep the box in a place where you and other people can reach it and put items inside that can be donated.

4. When your box is full, ask your teacher or an adult to help you take the items to a place where you can donate them.

Plan Your Donation Box

Name ________________

Tell About a Problem— Record a Video

Record a video to tell other people about a problem.

What You Need

- smartphone or other device that can record a video
- any objects you want to show or use in the video
- anything you want to wear in the video
- pencil
- index card

What You Do

1. Think about what you want to say about the problem in your video. Write it on the index card.

2. Gather objects or anything you want to use or show in the video.

3. Record yourself talking on the video. You can read from the index card if you'd like.

4. Show your video to someone.

Plan Your Video

You Can Learn from Mistakes

Diwa Learns a Lesson

This unit is about making mistakes and learning from them. Students will read a realistic fiction story about Diwa, a girl who did not tell her friends the rules at her house. Students may already have their own experiences with making a mistake and learning from it, so they may connect to Diwa's story, or they may learn anew the importance of mistakes as learning opportunities. As you guide students through these topics, consider their varying world views as they share their experiences and make connections to their own lives.

The pages in this unit are reproducible. Reproduce the unit in its entirety or choose the pages that you wish to have your students do. A suggested teaching path is below.

1. **Read the Realistic Fiction Story (pages 60 and 61)**

   Distribute one copy of the text to each student. Have students read the text independently, or read the text aloud as they follow along silently.

2. **Learning from Mistakes (page 62)**

   Distribute one copy of the page to each student. Guide students in completing the page independently.

3. **Let's Talk About the Story (page 63)**

   Distribute one copy of the page to each student. Facilitate a whole-group discussion or divide the class into small groups.

   Prepare for discussion:
   Tell students that they will have a conversation with classmates about the questions they have been given. Explain that they do not have to write complete answers to the questions. They can write notes about how they want to answer the questions or how they want to respond to other students' comments. Remind students that they can disagree with or add on to what other students say, as long as all students are respectful.

4. **Talk with Your Partner (pages 64 and 65)**

   Divide students into groups of two. Distribute one copy of each page to each group. Have each group work on the activity together.

5. **Choose Your Project—Always Learning (pages 66–70)**

   Distribute one copy of the project menu to each student. Explain to students that they will each choose a project to do. After students have chosen their project, collect the project menus.

   Reproduce and distribute one of the following project pages to each student based on the student's choice: Page 67 for the interview; Page 68 for the poem; Page 69 for the poster; Page 70 for the dance. Decide whether or not students will share their finished projects with the class and instruct students accordingly.

Diwa Learns a Lesson

Diwa gulped down her breakfast. She was so excited. Today her friends Kadeeja and Carly were coming over to her house for the first time. She couldn't wait to show them her bedroom and art supplies.

Finally, Diwa heard the doorbell ring. She ran to meet her friends at the door. "Come on!" Diwa said. She led Kadeeja and Carly to her room.

"Where are your dolls?" Kadeeja asked.

"Yeah, let's play dolls!" said Carly. "Ooo! Do you have a dollhouse or a doll car?"

"Um…yeah, I do. I just can't find them right now," said Diwa. Diwa didn't actually have any dolls or dollhouses or doll cars. She wasn't really interested in dolls. But now she wished she had some.

Diwa, Kadeeja, and Carly went downstairs, looking for something to do. They sat on the couch in the living room. Diwa was starting to get worried. Her friends looked so bored.

Then Kadeeja pointed to the little glass figurines on the mantle. "Wow!" she said. "Can we play with those?"

"That sounds fun!" said Carly.

Diwa didn't know what to do. The figurines were gifts from her grandfather. Some were animals. Some were people. All of them were fragile and special. Her mom brought them back from the Philippines the last time she went. Diwa knew she wasn't supposed to touch them. But her friends liked them so much.

"I guess so," said Diwa.

She took one down and handed it to Kadeeja. She took another one down and handed it to Carly. Then she reached up to grab one more figurine. It was a little horse. Just then, she heard her mom coming around the corner. Her hand slipped and she knocked the horse off the mantle. It hit the coffee table with a loud crack. The horse broke into two pieces.

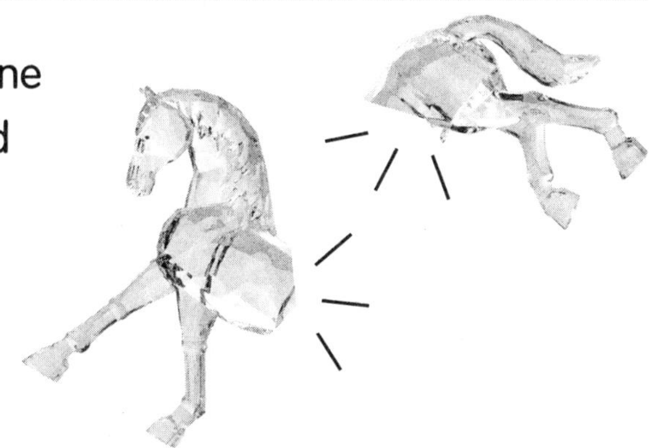

Diwa knelt down and started to cry. Diwa's mom came into the room. She picked up the pieces and collected the figurines from Kadeeja and Carly.

While Kadeeja and Carly had a snack in the kitchen, Diwa and her mom talked. Diwa was still crying. "I'm so sorry," she said through her tears.

Diwa's mom placed the figurines back on the mantle. She looked disappointed.

"I just didn't know how to say 'no' to my friends," said Diwa.

"I know it's hard," said Diwa's mom. "But it's important to be able to say 'no' when you need to."

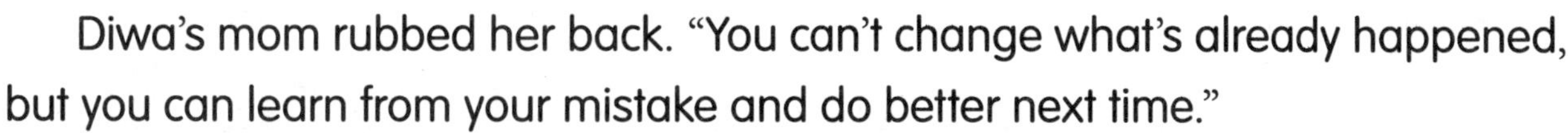

"I wish I'd made a different choice," said Diwa.

Diwa's mom rubbed her back. "You can't change what's already happened, but you can learn from your mistake and do better next time."

"Okay, Mom," Diwa said. "I will." She wiped her eyes. Then she joined her friends in the kitchen. She told them that she had not been honest before and that she was sorry. She explained that she didn't have any dolls and didn't really play with dolls much. "But I love art projects!" she said. It turned out they loved art projects, too. They spent the rest of the day painting and drawing together. When it was time to go, they all wished it didn't have to end.

Name _______________________

Learning from Mistakes

Diwa made a mistake when she let her friends play with the figurines. But she learned from her mistake. She learned to say "no" and to be honest with her friends.

Answer the items below about learning from mistakes.

1. Think about a mistake you made. It can be big or small.
   Draw a picture to show the mistake.

2. Now tell what you learned from the mistake.

____

____

____

____

____

____

   Culturally Responsive Lessons and Activities • EMC 8263 • © Evan-Moor Corporation

Name ___________________

Let's Talk About the Story

Read the questions. Think carefully about how to answer each one.
You will talk with classmates about your ideas. There are no wrong answers.
Below each question, you can write:

| Things that you want to say |  Things other people said that you agree with |  Things other people said that you disagree with |

1. Diwa had a hard time saying "no" to her friends. Why is it sometimes hard to say "no" to a friend?

2. Have you ever said "no" to a friend? Tell about it.

3. Are there some special things in your house that you're not supposed to play with? Tell about what those things are and why they are special.

4. Think of a sport or an activity that you like. When you first started learning that sport or activity, did you make mistakes? Tell about it.

Name _______________________

Name _______________________

Talk with Your Partner

1. With your partner, cut out the story cards.

2. Place the cards facedown in a stack.

3. Begin by having one partner take a card and read it aloud.

4. With your partner, talk about the person in the story whose name is underlined. Did this person make a mistake? Tell what you think this person could learn.

5. Then the next partner draws a card. Continue until you have read and talked about all the cards.

Guillo was first in line. Then Maxwell cut in front of him. Guillo shoved Maxwell. Maxwell shoved Guillo. Guillo fell backwards and accidentally hit his friend Samir in the face. Samir started crying.

On her walk to school, Ruby saw Alma. Alma had a new haircut. Ruby thought it looked weird. "That's a weird haircut," said Ruby. Alma didn't talk to her for the rest of the day.

Aliyah's family was going on a hike to a lake. Aliyah's parents told her to wear her jacket. But she didn't want to, so she left it behind. Soon, Aliyah started to feel cold and miserable. They had to go back early and never made it to the lake.

Jay saw some cool toy cars at his friend's house. He put one in his pocket when his friend wasn't looking. His friend didn't notice. But Jay felt sick to his stomach when he got home.

Olivia was supposed to do her homework. But she watched TV first and ran out of time. The next day, she was sad when her teacher collected homework and she didn't have hers.

Josiah's friends were being really loud in the library. Josiah didn't like it, but he didn't tell them to stop. Then the librarian came and told them they all had to leave.

Name_________________________

Name_________________________

Steps to Play the Game

1. Think about the story cards you read. With your partner, decide who learned the most important lesson and why. Complete the sentence below with the name and the reason the lesson was important.

_______________________ learned the most important lesson because _______________________

____.

2. Next, draw a scene showing how that character will behave in the future, now that he or she has learned this important lesson.

Name _______________________________

Choose Your Project— Always Learning

Diwa made a mistake, but she learned from it. She learned to say "no" and to be honest with her friends.

1. Think about mistakes you have made and what you have learned from them. Then choose a project to do from the menu below.

2. Write a ✓ to show which project you chose. Then give this page to your teacher.

☐ **Interview an Adult**

Ask an adult questions about how making mistakes can sometimes help us learn.

☐ **Write an Acrostic Poem**

Write a poem about making mistakes.

☐ **Make a Poster**

Make a poster that celebrates mistakes and all the ways they help us learn.

☐ **Do a Dance**

Record yourself doing a dance.

Name ___________________

Always Learning—Interview

Interview an adult about his or her experiences with learning from mistakes.
Ask the questions below and write the person's answers on the lines.

1. What is a sport or activity you like to do that was hard at first but has gotten easier?

____

When you first started that sport or activity, what kinds of mistakes did you make?

____

____

2. Can you think of any mistakes you made recently? _________________________

Tell me about one of these mistakes.

____

____

Did you learn anything from it?

____

____

3. Do you think mistakes are okay sometimes? Why or why not?

____

____

4. Do you think you will make more mistakes in the future? Why or why not?

____

____

Name ______________________

Always Learning—Acrostic Poem

Write a poem that tells why mistakes can be good in some ways.

What You Need

- light-colored construction paper
- markers or crayons

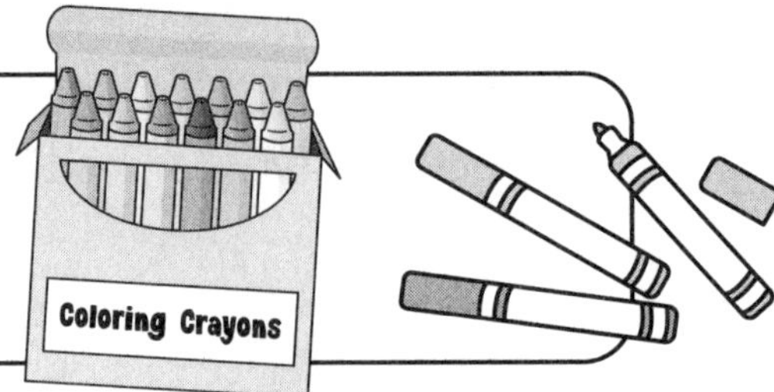

What You Do

1. Write the letters to spell the word **MISTAKE** from top to bottom on the left side of the paper.

2. Write a phrase that begins with each letter.

3. Draw pictures on the paper to make it colorful.

4. Share your poem with other people.

> **M**any people do it
> **I** can learn
> **S**
> **T**
> **A**
> **K**
> **E**

Plan Your Poem

 Culturally Responsive Lessons and Activities • EMC 8263 • © Evan-Moor Corporation

Name ___________________________

Always Learning—Poster

Use pictures and words to make a poster about mistakes and what they can teach us.

What You Need

- large sheet of construction paper
- materials to decorate the poster, such as colored pencils, paint, crayons, glue, glitter, scissors, colored tissue paper, cotton balls, buttons, beads, foil, etc.

What You Do

1. Think about mistakes people make and how we learn from them. Write a positive message about mistakes on your poster.
2. Draw pictures or symbols on the poster.
3. Decorate the poster.
4. Show your poster to your classmates.

Plan Your Poster

Name ______________________

Always Learning—Dance

Record a dance to show that mistakes do not have to keep us down and that we can still be happy even if we make mistakes sometimes.

What You Need

- smartphone or other device that can record a video
- music to play and dance to
- an outfit or any props to use in your dance

What You Do

1. Find a song to dance to.

2. Gather any props or put on any special clothing you want to wear in your dance.

3. If you want to, use the box below to plan your dance steps or moves before you do it. Or you can just dance from your heart and make up the moves as you go!

4. Record yourself dancing to the music or ask someone to help you record the video.

5. Watch the video to make sure you like it. You can record it again if you want to try again.

6. Show your video to other people.

Plan Your Dance

Culturally Responsive Lessons and Activities • EMC 8263 • © Evan-Moor Corporation

You Can Make New Friends

This unit is about making new friends and giving people a chance. Students will read a realistic fiction story about a boy named Jermaine, who connects a friend he already has with a new friend he makes. As you guide students through these topics, consider their varying world views as they share their experiences and make connections to their own lives.

The pages in this unit are reproducible. Reproduce the unit in its entirety or choose the pages that you wish to have your students do. A suggested teaching path is below.

1. **Read the Realistic Fiction Story (pages 72 and 73)**
   Distribute one copy of the text to each student. Have students read the text independently, or read the text aloud as they follow along silently.

2. **New Friends! (page 74)**
   Distribute one copy of the page to each student. Guide students in completing the page independently.

3. **Let's Talk About the Story (page 75)**
   Distribute one copy of the page to each student. Facilitate a whole-group discussion or divide the class into small groups.

   Prepare for discussion:
   Tell students that they will have a conversation with classmates about the questions they have been given. Explain that they do not have to write complete answers to the questions. They can write notes about how they want to answer the questions or how they want to respond to other students' comments. Remind students that they can disagree with or add on to what other students say, as long as all students are respectful.

4. **Talk with Your Partner (pages 76 and 77)**
   Divide students into groups of two. Distribute one copy of each page to each group. Have each group work on the activity together.

5. **Choose Your Project—Making Friends (pages 78–82)**
   Distribute one copy of the project menu to each student. Explain to students that they will each choose a project to do. After students have chosen their project, collect the project menus.

   Reproduce and distribute one of the following project pages to each student based on the student's choice: Page 79 for the card; Page 80 for the video; Page 81 for the list; Page 82 for the poem. Decide whether or not students will share their finished projects with the class and instruct students accordingly.

Name _______________________

We Can All Be Friends

"Jermaine, pay attention!" said Chase. "Recess is almost over. You keep missing my passes, and then it takes forever for us to go find the ball and bring it back!" Jermaine and Chase were on the field, like every recess, passing the football back and forth to each other. Even though Jermaine liked football, he wanted to try doing something else at recess sometimes.

"Maybe we can try playing four square next time," Jermaine said, just as the bell rang. With a grunt, Chase ran over to the recess bucket, threw the football in, and lined up with the rest of his classmates. Jermaine was right behind him.

Later, the class was in P.E. The teacher said that the students were going to practice doing passes. She pulled out a bucket of footballs and told everyone to find a partner. "Yesssss!" said Chase and Jermaine at the same time. Of course, they knew they were going to be partners.

They found the perfect spot on the field. As Jermaine was getting ready to do his first throw, he noticed that Bingwen looked kind of lost. Without even thinking, Jermaine said, "Hey, Bingwen, come and throw with us!" For a second, Jermaine wasn't sure that Bingwen heard him because he looked surprised. But he nodded and started to run over.

Jermaine looked at Chase, who was frowning. "Why did you ask him? He never throws the football at recess or after school. He won't be good at passing. I don't want to play with him."

Jermaine just waved his arm at Chase to show that he thought Chase was talking nonsense. "We don't know that he won't be good at it!"

The three boys threw the ball to each other. They laughed a lot and talked a little as they passed the ball, and before they knew it, P.E. was over. That meant it was lunchtime!

Every third-grade class had its own lunch table. Even though Bingwen was in the same class as Chase and Jermaine, he never sat with them before. He always sat with Miguel and Brian. Today, Chase was buying lunch, so it took him longer to get to the lunch table. And he was in for a surprise when he got there! Instead of sitting in his usual spot at the end of the table, Jermaine was sitting in the middle with Bingwen and his friends. "Hey, Chase! I saved you a spot here!" said Jermaine.

Chase shook his head and just stood holding his lunch. It was like he was expecting Jermaine to get up and move. But Jermaine stayed seated where he was. So Chase just shrugged and sat down with Jermaine.

"You did pretty well with the football," Jermaine said to Bingwen, before stuffing potato chips into his mouth. "You should come throw with us at recess sometimes."

"I usually play four square," said Bingwen. "You gotta try it. It's probably my favorite game."

Chase saw Jermaine nodding and smiling big. "Can I come play four square, too?" Chase asked quietly.

"Of course!" said Bingwen. "Hey, you guys gotta try these. They're mini pineapple tarts that my mom makes. They're a Chinese dessert. I get them in my lunch every day."

"These are so good!" said Jermaine. "I never had a Chinese dessert before. Are you Chinese?" Bingwen nodded and smiled. Jermaine and Chase smiled back. All the boys knew that they had just made a new friend.

Name ______________________________

     # New Friends!     

Jermaine was friendly and made a new friend. He wanted to be friends with Bingwen, but he still wanted to be friends with Chase, too.

Answer the items below about making friends.

1. Draw or write to tell about a time that you made a new friend.

2. Read the words inside the circles. Color the ones that tell something that is hard about making new friends.

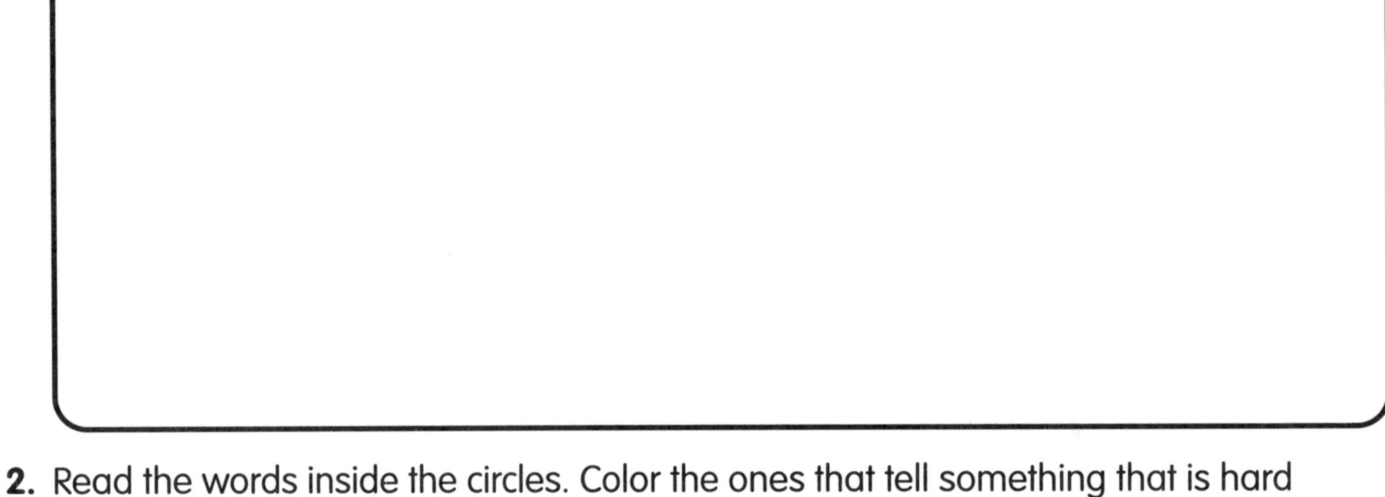

3. Write one thing that is good about making new friends.

____

   Culturally Responsive Lessons and Activities • EMC 8263 • © Evan-Moor Corporation

Name ______________________________

   # Let's Talk About the Story   

Read the questions. Think carefully about how to answer each one.
You will talk with classmates about your ideas. There are no wrong answers.
Below each question, you can write:

| Things that you want to say |  | Things other people said that you agree with |  | Things other people said that you disagree with |

1. Do you think it is easy or hard to make new friends? Tell why you have your opinion.

2. In the story, Chase didn't want to give Bingwen a chance to throw the football with him and Jermaine. Why should a person give another person a chance?

3. Would you be friends with someone only if your old friends like that person? Why or why not?

4. What makes a person a good friend?

Name _______________________

Name _______________________

Talk with Your Partner

Jermaine and Chase found out that they can make a new friend and still be friends with each other. Below is a script for a play. Decide with your partner who will read the part of Aurelia and who will read the part of Shaquana. Then answer the items on page 77 with your partner.

Aurelia	Why did you let Daisy use your jacket at recess? Are you friends with her now?
Shaquana	I guess. She's nice, and she said she was really cold.
Aurelia	Yeah, but we never talked to her much before. She's in a different class.
Shaquana	Yeah, but she lives in our neighborhood, and she rides the same school bus as we do. We could start talking to her more.
Aurelia	Well, maybe you just want to be friends with her then. I don't have to be your friend anymore.
Shaquana	Or we could all be friends. We don't just have to keep the same friends all the time without making new friends. We can always make new friends, too. And you should talk to Daisy, because she's nice.
Aurelia	I don't think she would let me ever use her jacket if I were cold.
Shaquana	I bet she would. She is really cool. And she has that new kind of lunchbox you have been wanting your mom to get you. She showed it to me. She'll probably show you if you ask her.
Aurelia	Really? I didn't know that. I do want to see it!
Shaquana	Let's sit by her on the bus this afternoon.
Aurelia	Okay, we can sit by her. But if you get on the bus first, you'd better save me a spot, too!
Shaquana	Of course! I'll save both of you spots if I get on the bus first!

Name ___________________________________

Name ___________________________________

Answer the items with your partner.

1. Do you think that Aurelia was giving Daisy a chance?
Tell why you think so or why you do not.

____

____

____

2. Who do you think you are most like: Aurelia or Shaquana?
Write your answers and tell why in the circles.

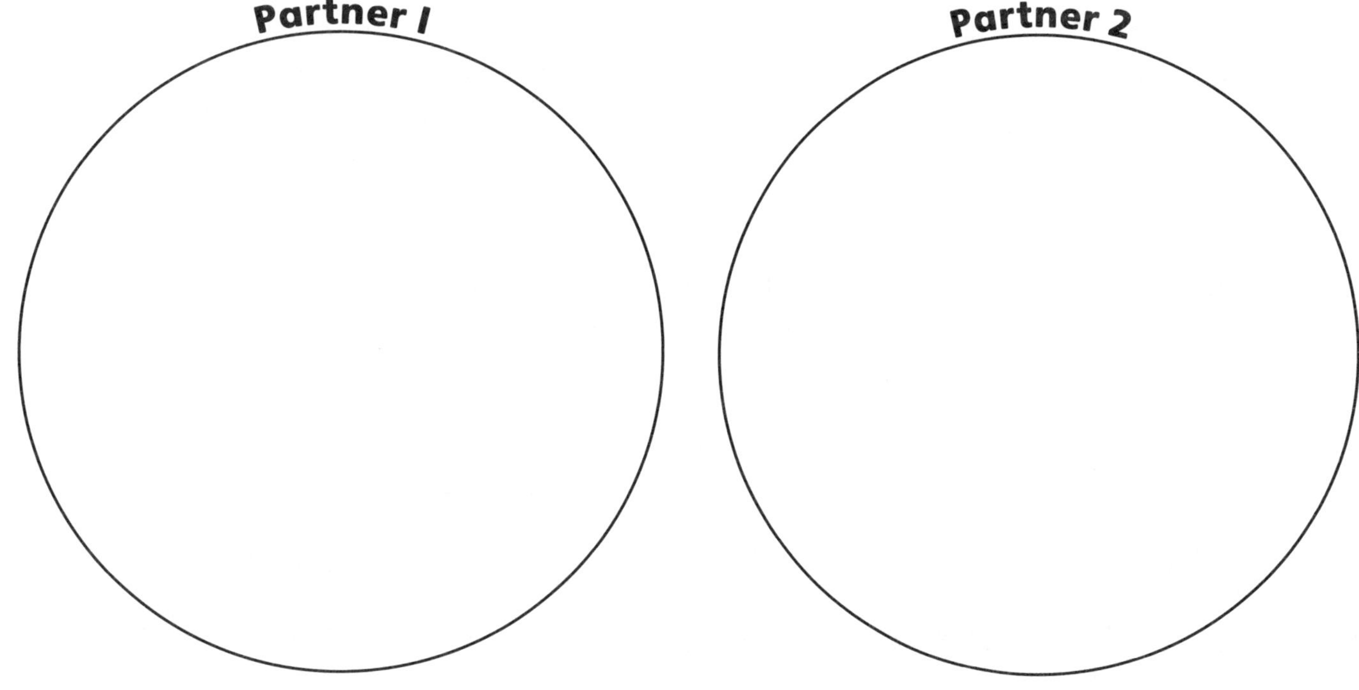

3. Would you rather be friends with Shaquana or Aurelia? Why?

____

____

____

Name ___________________________

Choose Your Project— Making Friends

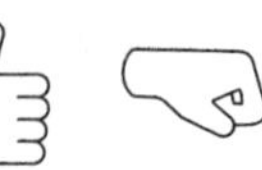

Jermaine and Chase learned that they can make new friends if they are willing to give other people a chance. They also learned that when they make new friends, they can still have fun with the friends they already have.

1. Think about what it's like to make new friends. Then choose a project to do from the menu below.

2. Write a ✓ to show which project you chose. Then give this page to your teacher.

☐ **Make a Card**

Make a card for someone that says "Let's Be Friends!"

☐ **Record a Video**

Use a smartphone or device to record a video that shows one way to make new friends.

☐ **Write a List**

Write a big list that tells reasons why it's good to have a friend or friends.

☐ **Write an Acrostic Poem**

Write a poem about friendship.

Name ___________________

Making Friends—Make a Card

Make a card that lets someone know that you want to be friends.

What You Need

- sheet of light-colored construction paper
- crayons or markers
- materials to decorate the card, such as glue, pompoms, glitter, paint, cotton balls, foil, beads, colored tissue paper, stamps, etc.

What You Do

1. Fold the construction paper in half so that it folds open like a greeting card.
2. Write a message inside the card that tells someone that you want to be friends. Write your name in the card to tell who it is from.
3. Decorate the card.
4. Give your card to someone or share your card with your friends.

Plan Your Card

Name _______________________

Making Friends—Record a Video

Record a video to show one way to make new friends.

What You Need

- smartphone or other device that can record a video
- any objects you want to wear or use in the video, or music
- index card
- pencil

What You Do

1. On the index card, write what you want to say or do in your video.

2. Record your video. You can read from the index card as you make the video.

3. Share your video with your class.

Culturally Responsive Lessons and Activities • EMC 8263 • © Evan-Moor Corporation

Name ___________________________

Making Friends—Write a List

Write and decorate a list that tells what you like about friendship.

What You Need

- light-colored construction paper
- markers or colored pencils
- materials to decorate the list, such as paint, crayons, glue, glitter, scissors, colored tissue paper, cotton balls, buttons, beads, foil, etc.

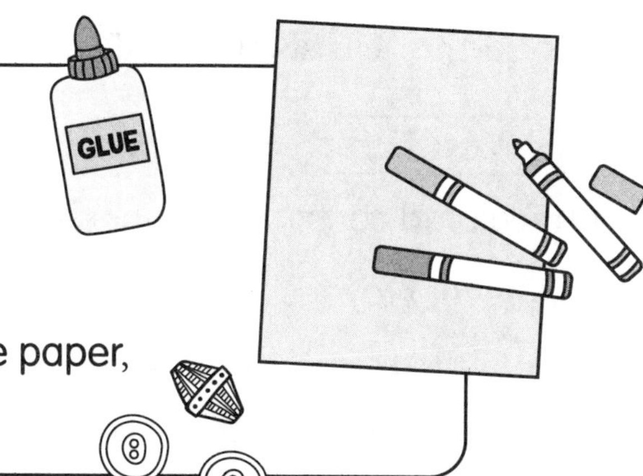

What You Do

1. Write a list of at least 4 reasons why it is good to have a friend or friends.
2. Hang up your list or show your list to other people.

Plan Your List

Name ___________________

Making Friends—
Write an Acrostic Poem

Write a poem that tells about friendship.

What You Need

- light-colored construction paper
- markers or crayons
- materials to decorate the poem, such as colored pencils, paint, glue, glitter, scissors, colored tissue paper, cotton balls, buttons, beads, foil, etc.

What You Do

1. Write the letters to spell the word **FRIEND** from top to bottom on the left side of the paper.

2. Write your own phrase about friendship that begins with each letter.

3. Decorate the poem.

4. Give your poem to someone or show it to your friends.

Fun
Reading each other's messages
In school or at home
E
N
D

Plan Your Poem

Culturally Responsive Lessons and Activities • EMC 8263 • © Evan-Moor Corporation

Let Other People Show What They Can Do

Movie Project

This unit is about respecting others by not making assumptions about them. Students will read a realistic fiction story about Deshawn, a boy who made assumptions about what his classmate, Izaak, can do because Izaak is in a wheelchair. We can learn more about others when we do not make assumptions about their abilities. As you guide students through these topics, consider their varying world views as they share their experiences and make connections to their own lives.

The pages in this unit are reproducible. Reproduce the unit in its entirety or choose the pages that you wish to have your students do. A suggested teaching path is below.

1. **Read the Realistic Fiction Story (pages 84 and 85)**
   Distribute one copy of the text to each student. Have students read the text independently, or read the text aloud as they follow along silently.

2. **Jumping to Conclusions (page 86)**
   Guide students in completing the page independently. You may decide to have a class discussion afterward so students can share their different interpretations of each photograph. Helping students analyze the conclusions drawn by classmates may lead to a rich discussion about first impressions and quick judgments.

3. **Let's Talk About the Story (page 87)**
   Distribute one copy of the page to each student. Facilitate a whole-group discussion or divide the class into small groups.

   Prepare for discussion:
   Tell students that they will have a conversation with classmates about the questions they have been given. Explain that they do not have to write complete answers to the questions. They can write notes about how they want to answer the questions or how they want to respond to other students' comments. Remind students that they can disagree with or add on to what other students say, as long as all students are respectful.

4. **Talk with Your Partner (pages 88 and 89)**
   Divide students into groups of two. Distribute one copy of each page to each group. Have each group work on the activity together.

5. **Choose Your Project—Respect Others (pages 90–94)**
   Distribute one copy of the project menu to each student. Explain to students that they will each choose a project to do. After students have chosen their project, collect the project menus.

   Reproduce and distribute one of the following project pages to each student based on the student's choice: Page 91 for the poster; Page 92 for the coloring page; Page 93 for the skit; Page 94 for the checklist. Decide whether or not students will share their finished projects with the class and instruct students accordingly.

Movie Project

Mrs. Cruz closed the book with a snap. Her students started chattering about the unexpected ending to the story. She raised her hand until they quieted again.

"Your job is to work with your partner to create a video book report about the story," she explained. "Did you like the ending? If not, create a new ending in your video. Your partner's name is listed on the board."

Deshawn looked up at the partner list and frowned. Oh no. Izaak. How could he work with Izaak? Deshawn already had some great ideas about the video, but he didn't think Izaak would be the most helpful partner.

Before lunch, Deshawn approached Mrs. Cruz's desk and whispered, "I don't know how to work with Izaak."

"What do you mean?" she smiled, looking up from her computer.

"I wanted to make an action video."

"Sounds exciting," she said. "I'm sure you both can figure it out."

"But he can't do, I mean, he can't…" Deshawn struggled to say what he was thinking.

"Oh," sighed Mrs. Cruz, "you are worried about Izaak's wheelchair?"

"Well, yeah," said Deshawn.

"Why don't you politely ask Izaak about his wheelchair? I'm sure he'd be happy to explain. He is fully able to be your partner." She clapped her hands for the class to line up.

The next day, Mrs. Cruz planned time for partners to work together on the book report. Deshawn and Izaak got to work outside the classroom at a big table. Izaak's wheelchair fit better there.

"So, what do you want to do?" Izaak spoke up first.

Deshawn looked down at Izaak's neon shoelaces neatly tied. He wondered, "Can Izaak tie his own laces, or did someone else help him?"

"I want to make a new ending to the story," Deshawn started, "but I wanted to have the boys racing against each other at the end."

"Why not? I like that idea!"

Deshawn and Izaak talked about more of their ideas, and Deshawn was glad to know that Izaak also really liked action movies. They agreed on almost everything.

"So, Izaak," Deshawn said after a while. "Do you feel comfortable racing me, even though you are in a wheelchair? Is that going to be okay for you to do?"

Izaak laughed. "I'm glad you asked. I love racing. And my motor chair can go faster than you can walk, I bet!"

Deshawn's eyes got bigger. "That's awesome!" he said.

During the next week, the boys worked on their project together. Deshawn borrowed his mom's smartphone, and he went over to Izaak's house on Saturday so they could record the video. Then they showed their video to the class the following week. Everybody loved it!

"I think we made a great team, Izaak," Deshawn said. "I'm sorry that I wasn't sure that you could make the video with me, at first. I was wrong to make guesses about you like that."

"That's okay," Izaak said. "Most people think I can't do anything because I'm in a wheelchair!" He rolled his eyes.

"Well, I won't make that mistake again," said Deshawn. "Hey, do you want to come over to my house next Saturday to watch a real action movie?"

🔗 Jumping to Conclusions 🔗

A conclusion is a judgment or an opinion that you make about someone or something. The phrase "jump to conclusions" means you make a quick judgment. Quick guesses are not always correct, though. Look at the photos and try to guess what is happening. Things may not always be as they seem.

1. Explain what you think is happening: Why are these children sitting? What might they be thinking or feeling? Do they look happy to you?

Staff Sgt. Andrew Smith (U.S Army Photographer)

____

____

____

____

2. Explain what you think is happening: Why is the boy sweating? Is he focusing on something? Is he having a good time, a bad time, or neither good nor bad?

____

____

____

____

3. Explain what you think is happening: How do you think the girl feels? What would make her outdoor time more fun?

____

____

____

____

Name ______________________

Let's Talk About the Story

Read the questions. Think carefully about how to answer each one.
You will talk with classmates about your ideas. There are no wrong answers.
Below each question, you can write:

| Things that you want to say | Things other people said that you agree with | Things other people said that you disagree with |

1. Think of a time when someone jumped to a conclusion about you. How did you feel?

2. When you meet a person who walks, talks, or looks different from you, how might you try to get to know that person?

3. Do you think that you ever jump to conclusions? Why or why not?

4. Do you think Deshawn was fair to Izaak at the beginning of the story? Tell what you think and why.

Name ______________________

Name ______________________

Talk with Your Partner

The sentences below are examples of jumping to conclusions. Cut out the cards on page 89 and give one of each to each person. Then, with your partner, read the statements below. After you read each one, say "3, 2, 1, Jump!" Then jump into the air and hold up the card that tells if you agree or disagree with the conclusion in the statement.

1. Krishna is not smiling. He must be sad or upset.

2. Travis comes to school with holes in his shoes. His family does not have money to buy him new shoes.

3. Bryce was late coming back from recess. Something must be wrong.

4. Pearl didn't get excited when I told her about my trip to Disney World. She must not like me anymore.

5. Kai sees a police car in front of his neighbor's house. He thinks to himself, "The people next door did something bad!"

6. Everyone will have a great time at Yani's house because she has a trampoline!

7. Jamila uses crutches to help her walk. She probably won't be able to go on the field trip because of that.

8. Leon must be mad at me. He doesn't sit next to me at lunch anymore.

9. Aziz just moved here from India. He is new at school. He probably cannot speak English very well.

10. We should have chocolate ice cream for Naomi's birthday because everyone loves chocolate ice cream.

11. I heard that the new P.E. teacher is really mean. I wish I didn't have to go to P.E. today.

Agree

Agree

Disagree

Disagree

Name _______________________

Choose Your Project—
Respect Others

Deshawn made an incorrect guess about what Izaak could do just because of Izaak's wheelchair. Deshawn said he was sorry and learned to ask friendly questions rather than jump to conclusions.

1. Think about what it means to not jump to conclusions about other people. Then choose a project to do from the menu below.

2. Write a ✓ to show which project you chose. Then give this page to your teacher.

☐ **Lift-the-Flap Poster**

Make a poster with photos and a hidden story under each photo.

☐ **Coloring Page**

Color a picture using key words and phrases about giving people a chance and not jumping to conclusions.

☐ **Act Out a Skit**

Act in a short scene with a partner to show ways to be respectful to others.

☐ **Make a Checklist**

Make a checklist of things for you to remember to help you be respectful when you meet someone new.

Culturally Responsive Lessons and Activities • EMC 8263 • © Evan-Moor Corporation

Respect Others—Lift-the-Flap Poster

Choose 4 photographs that show people in your family or community. Write about what is happening in each photo. Other people can make guesses about the photos.

What You Need

- 4 photographs that each show something different
- poster board and colored construction paper
- tape
- glue
- scissors
- lined paper for writing
- pencil or pen

What You Do

1. Choose 4 photos that tell a story.

2. Glue each photo to a piece of construction paper, leaving a little room above the photo for tape.

3. Tape the top of each piece of construction paper to the poster board.

4. Cut 4 pieces of lined writing paper to fit under the construction paper pieces. Write what is happening in each photo. Then tape the lined paper under each flap.

5. Show your poster to other people and let them guess what is happening in the photos. Then they can lift the flaps to read if they guessed right or learn what is really happening in each photo.

Name ___________________

Respect Others—Coloring Page

Read the words in the picture. Color the positive and respectful words and phrases green. Color the negative and disrespectful words and phrases blue. What picture did you create?

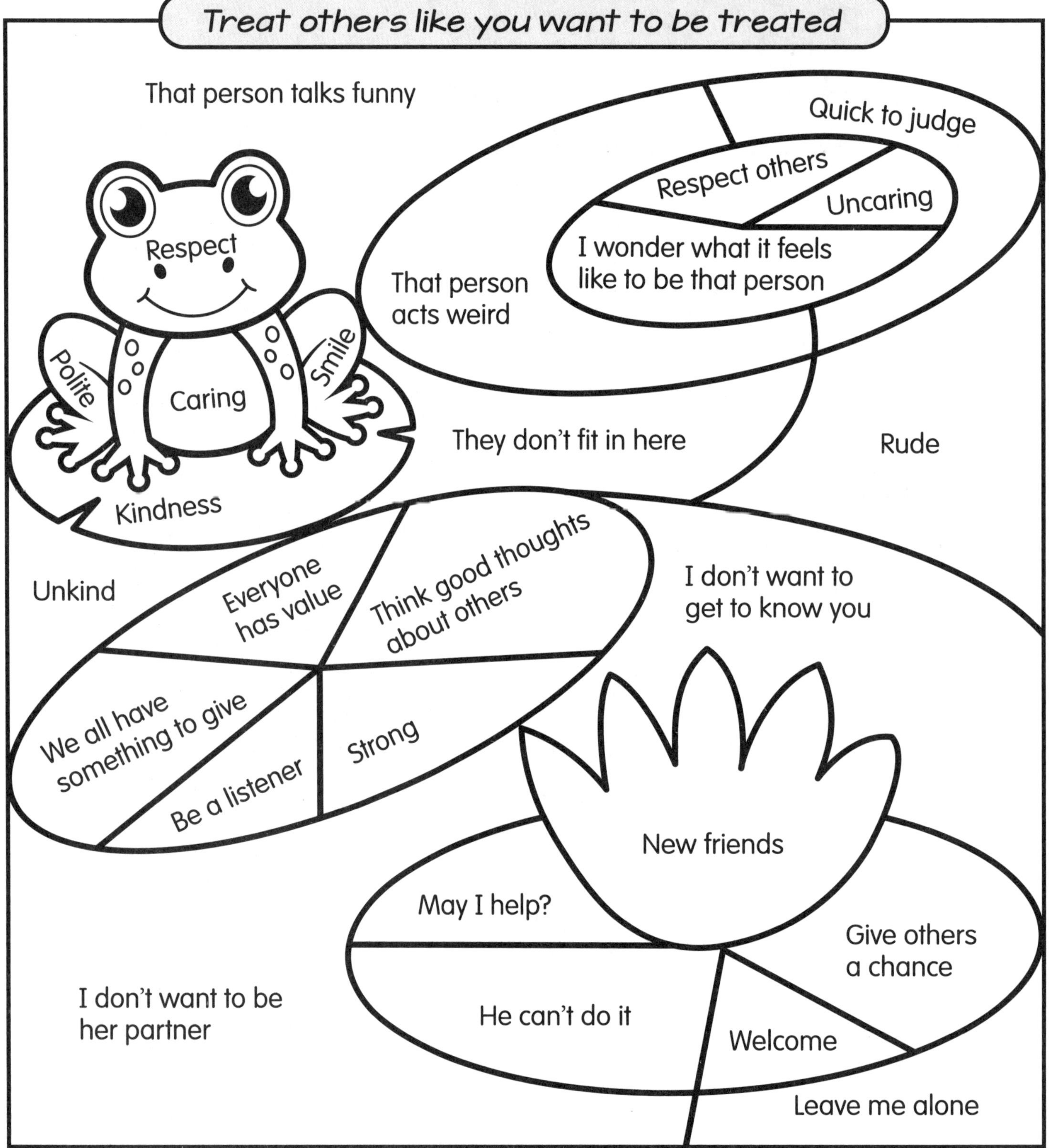

Name _______________________

Respect Others—Act Out a Skit

Act out a short skit to show one way that you can show respect to other people.

What You Need

- a partner
- paper and pencil
- any equipment or props to act out the skit

What You Do

1. Think of one way that you can show respect to others. Think about how you would act that out and what you would say or do. Or think of a problem where someone is not being respectful and how to help that person learn, like Deshawn did in the story.

2. Write what you will do or say in the skit. Write what the other person will do or say. Then find a partner to help you act out the skit.

3. Practice acting out the skit.

4. Show your skit to someone or use a device to record you and your partner acting out the skit.

Plan Your Skit

Name _______________________

Respect Others—Checklist

Make a checklist of 5 things you can do to show respect to other people.

What You Need

- sheet of colored construction paper
- markers or colored pencils
- materials to decorate the checklist, such as glitter, cotton balls, glue, colored tissue paper, dried pasta, stamps, beads, paint, etc.

What You Do

1. On the construction paper, write a list of 5 things you can do to show respect to other people. You may also choose to write things to NOT do.
2. Decorate the checklist.
3. Hang your checklist somewhere you will be able to see it often.

Plan Your Checklist

Culturally Responsive Lessons and Activities • EMC 8263 • © Evan-Moor Corporation

It's Better When We Work Together

Let's Dance Together: A Retelling of Ananse and the Pot

This unit is about cooperation and community. It's about how things turn out better when people work together as a team. Students will read a modern retelling of "Ananse and the Pot," an African folk tale about the value of sharing your wisdom with others. Students may learn how you can help other people by teaching them, or they might realize that you also help yourself when you help others. As you guide students through these topics, consider their varying world views as they share their experiences and make connections to their own lives.

The pages in this unit are reproducible. Reproduce the unit in its entirety or choose the pages that you wish to have your students do. A suggested teaching path is below.

1. **Read the Realistic Fiction Story (pages 96 and 97)**

   Distribute one copy of the text to each student. Have students read the text independently, or read the text aloud as they follow along silently.

2. **Working with Others (page 98)**

   Distribute one copy of the page to each student. Guide students in completing the page independently.

3. **Let's Talk About the Story (page 99)**

   Distribute one copy of the page to each student. Facilitate a whole-group discussion or divide the class into small groups.

   Prepare for discussion:
   Tell students that they will have a conversation with classmates about the questions they have been given. Explain that they do not have to write complete answers to the questions. They can write notes about how they want to answer the questions or how they want to respond to other students' comments. Remind students that they can disagree with or add on to what other students say, as long as all students are respectful.

4. **Talk with Your Partner and Team Dance (pages 100 and 101)**

   Divide students into groups of two. Distribute one copy of each page to each group. Have each group work on the activities together.

5. **Choose Your Project—Working Together (pages 102–106)**

   Distribute one copy of the project menu to each student. Explain to students that they will each choose a project to do. After students have chosen their project, collect the project menus.

   Reproduce and distribute one of the following project pages to each student based on the student's choice: Page 103 for the painting; Page 104 for the poster; Page 105 for the photo album; Page 106 for the song. Decide whether or not students will share their finished projects with the class and instruct students accordingly.

Name ______________________________

Let's Dance Together

Kai was in the spotlight. Again.

"Watch me, everyone!" Kai danced to the music. She moved with rhythm.

"Bravo, Kai!" said their teacher, Ms. Liu. "Perfect!"

Ms. Liu's third-grade class was getting ready for their big musical. Everyone had a role. But some people were better at dancing. They had bigger roles. Kai was one of them.

"I can't do any of these dance moves," Juan whispered to Jill.

"Me neither," Jill said, shaking her head. Jill was very tall. She usually loved being tall. Everyone could see her. But she felt shy about her dancing skills.

Juan was short. He moved fast on the basketball court. But he couldn't seem to dance. He kept tripping over his own feet.

Kai was still dancing. She made dancing look easy. Jill and Juan looked at each other. "What if we asked Kai for help?" Jill said.

They went over to Kai. "What do you want?" she asked.

Jill felt nervous. "We…we wanted to know if you could help us."

"You seem to know a lot about dancing," Juan added. "Could you give us some tips?"

Kai frowned. "I'm the dance master," she said. "If I help you two get better at dancing, I won't be the dance master anymore."

"We aren't very good," Jill said. "You will still be the dance master."

"I like being in the spotlight," Kai said. "I don't want to share the spotlight with anyone." She walked away.

Jill and Juan sat down on the ground. Their heads hung low. "We are never going to figure out this dance," Jill said sadly.

"Why don't I help you two out?" a voice said. Jill and Juan looked up. It was Kamala. She was the new kid in their class. Kamala sat next to them. She grinned. "I'm not as good a dancer as Kai, but I love to dance. It's my favorite thing in the world! Maybe I can help you two practice."

Kamala held out her hands to Jill and Juan. "Come on! I'll show you two some dance tricks."

"Are you sure you want to help us?" asked Juan. "We're not the best."

"Of course I do!" Kamala smiled. "My mom says things turn out better when we help each other and work together."

Jill and Juan smiled back. Kamala was so excited to help them. It made them feel like they could do anything. The three students practiced all afternoon. Kamala showed them how to do each dance step. Jill and Juan got better and better. Ms. Liu even noticed. "You two have improved so much!" she said.

It was then the night of the musical. Kai danced in the spotlight. She was still the dance master. But after the musical was over, people went to see Kamala, Jill, and Juan. "You three looked like you had so much fun!" one parent said. "You moved together as a team."

Jill, Juan, and Kamala grinned. "We all learned a lot from each other," Kamala said. "Jill showed me how to stand taller. And Juan taught me how to move quickly!"

Juan nodded. "We're better together!"

Jill, Juan, and Kamala felt so proud of themselves after the show. They were now teammates—and friends for life.

Name _______________________

Working with Others

Kamala, Jill, and Juan had different talents. They all taught each other something new. They worked together. Write or draw to tell 3 ways you work together with others.

 This is one way I work together with others at home.

 This is one way I work together with others in my classroom.

 This is one way I work together with others on the playground.

Culturally Responsive Lessons and Activities • EMC 8263 • © Evan-Moor Corporation

Name _______________________

 # Let's Talk About the Story 

Read the questions. Think carefully about how to answer each one.
You will talk with classmates about your ideas. There are no wrong answers.
Below each question, you can write:

| Things that you want to say |  | Things other people said that you agree with |  | Things other people said that you disagree with |

1. What do you think of what Kai said when Juan and Jill asked her for help?

2. Which character in the story is most like you? Which one is least like you? Tell why.

3. Why do you think things turned out better for Juan, Jill, and Kamala when they worked together?

Name _______________________

Name _______________________

 # Talk with Your Partner 

Jill, Juan, and Kamala helped each other. When they worked together, they all became better dancers. Talk with your partner about why things turn out better when people work together. Then draw or write your own ideas in the blank puzzle pieces.

Why Do We Work Together?

When we work together, we…

can solve problems as a team.

When we work together, we…

can have fun!

When we work together, we…

come up with more ideas.

When we work together, we…

When we work together, we…

When we work together, we…

Name _______________________

Name _______________________

Team Dance

Kamala, Juan, and Jill worked as a team. They learned how to dance together. This activity can help you and your partner work together to make your own dance.

1. Find music to play and dance to. Pick a song that you both like.

2. Plan your dance steps or moves first. Think of one dance move. Write it down. Then ask your partner to think of the next dance move. Write it down.

3. Keep going until you and your partner have 6 dance moves. Cut out your dance plan. Practice your dance together. Then show your dance to your friends!

Our Team's Dance

Partner 1 (Name)	Partner 2 (Name)
①	①
②	②
③	③

Name _______________________

Choose Your Project— Working Together

Kamala, Juan, and Jill worked together as a team.

1. Think about how you feel and how things turn out when you work together with others. Choose a project to do from the menu below.

2. Write a ✓ to show which project you chose. Then give this page to your teacher.

☐ **Make a Painting**

Paint a picture that shows how you work together with others.

☐ **Make a Poster**

Cut and paste pictures and words onto a poster to show how you work together with others.

☐ **Make a Photo Album**

Make a photo album with photos of you working together with others.

☐ **Record a Song**

Record yourself singing a song with a friend.

Culturally Responsive Lessons and Activities • EMC 8263 • © Evan-Moor Corporation

Name _______________________

Working Together—Painting

Paint a picture showing how you can work together with others.

What You Need

- large sheet of construction paper
- paints
- paintbrush

What You Do

1. Use the paintbrush and paints to paint your picture of you working with others.

2. Let your painting dry.

3. Show your painting to your friends.

Plan Your Painting

Name _______________________

Working Together—Poster

Make a poster with words and pictures to show how you work together with others.

What You Need

- large sheet of construction paper
- crayons or markers
- glue or tape
- scissors
- magazines or pictures that you can cut out
- things to decorate the poster, such as dried pasta, beads, buttons, cotton balls, paint, glitter, pompoms, dried leaves, foil, etc.

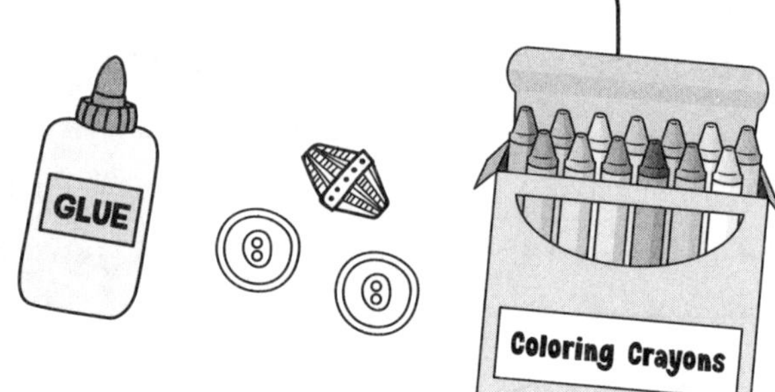

What You Do

1. Cut out pictures that show how you work together with others.
2. Glue or tape the pictures onto the construction paper.
3. Write your own words to tell about how you work together with others.
4. Add decorations to your poster.
5. Show your poster to your friends.

Plan Your Poster

Culturally Responsive Lessons and Activities • EMC 8263 • © Evan-Moor Corporation

Name _______________________

Working Together—Photo Album

Make a photo album with photographs that show how you work together with others.

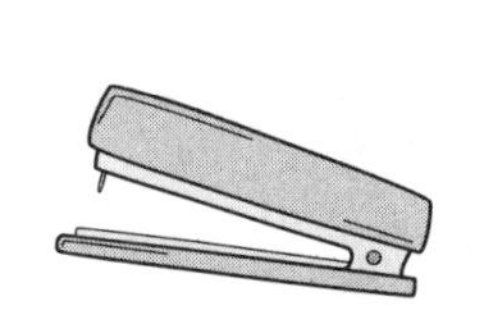

What You Need

- smartphone or other device to take photos
- stapler
- 2 sheets of light-colored construction paper
- glue or tape
- pen or marker
- materials to decorate the photo album, such as glitter, dried pasta, cotton balls, colored tissue paper, beads, buttons, foil, etc.

What You Do

1. Take or find photos that show you working together with other people.
2. Place the 2 sheets of construction paper on top of each other. Fold them in half like a book. Then staple them together on the left side.
3. Glue or tape the photos inside the photo album.
4. Decorate the cover of your photo album. Then show it to someone.

Plan Your Photo Album

Name _______________________

Working Together—Song

Record you and your friend singing a song together.

What You Need

- smartphone or other device that can record a video
- an outfit or any props to use as you and your friend sing
- a song to sing

What You Do

1. Find a song that you and your friend want to sing. Find the words to the song. Write them down or print them out.

2. Use a smartphone or a device to record a video or just the sound of you and your friend singing the song. If you choose to make a video, you and your friend can use props or wear special outfits.

3. Watch or listen to the recording. You can record it again if you want to.

4. After you finish your recording, share it with others.

Plan Your Song

Let's Celebrate Who We Are

This unit is about your students. The goal of this unit is to foster a sense of belonging for every student. Every student deserves to feel safe and proud when sharing about his or her own culture and life. When we talk about culture in this unit, we are not only referring to students' ethnic or national cultures, but also their social cultures, which includes students' values, stories, traditions, interests, struggles, and more. One way to help all students feel a sense of belonging is for them to share about themselves and learn about each other.

The pages in this unit are reproducible. Reproduce the unit in its entirety or choose the pages that you wish to have your students do.

1. **Let's Talk About Culture (page 108)**

   Distribute one copy of the page to each student. Facilitate a whole-group discussion or divide the class into small groups. Explain to students that they do not have to write complete answers to the questions. They can write notes about what they would like to say during the discussion.

2. **Heads Down, Palms Up! (pages 109 and 110)**

   Distribute one copy of the activity page and one copy of the fact cards on page 110 to each student. Provide students with the other materials needed for this activity and facilitate the game.

3. **This Makes Me Happy (page 111)**

   Distribute one copy of the page to each student. Provide the materials needed for the activity.

4. **Same and Different Handprints (page 112)**

   Distribute one copy of the page to each student. Provide the materials needed for the activity. Plan the space where you will display the handprints for students to compare and contrast.

5. **Give Shout-outs! (pages 113 and 114)**

   Distribute one copy of each page to each student. Provide the materials needed for the activity.

6. **Questions for Parent/Guardian and A Bit About Me, A Bit About You (pages 115 and 116)**

   Distribute one copy of page 115 to each student. This page is for students to take home. After students return the page to you, use the answers to form questions to ask each student during the circle discussion for A Bit About Me, A Bit About You. Before beginning the discussion, distribute the appropriate number of copies of page 116 to each student.

7. **Do You Agree? (pages 117 and 118)**

   Cut out the sentences on page 118. Then distribute one copy of the activity page and one sentence to each student. Reproduce multiple copies of the sentences as needed. Provide the other materials needed for the activity.

Name _______________________

Let's Talk About Culture

Read the questions. Think carefully about how to answer each one.
You will talk with classmates about your ideas. There are no wrong answers.
Below each question, you can write:

Things that you want to say  Things other people said that you agree with  Things other people said that you disagree with

1. Every person is different from other people, but all people are the same in many ways, too. Do you think it is good or not good that every person is so different from everyone else?

2. Do you believe that all people can choose to be kind or mean? Tell what you believe and why.

3. What are some of the ways that all people are the same, no matter where they live or what they look like?

4. What are some of the things that make you and your family different from other families?

Name _______________________

Heads Down, Palms Up!

Play a fun game and learn about your classmates at the same time.

What You Need

- clear desktop or tabletop space and chair for each player
- fact cards on page 110
- scissors
- small baggie for each player

What You Do

1. Write a fact about yourself on each card on page 110. Then cut out the cards and put them into the baggie without showing anybody what you wrote. Keep the baggie with you.

2. The teacher will choose 5 players to stand at the front of the classroom. All other players must close their eyes, put their head down on the desktop or tabletop, and stretch one hand out with the palm facing up.

3. Each of the 5 standing players will take one of the fact cards he or she wrote and place it in the palm of a sitting player. Then the 5 players return to their places at the front of the room. The sitting players must keep their eyes closed until the teacher instructs them to sit up and open their eyes.

4. When the sitting players open their eyes, those with a card read it and stand up. Then they each get one turn to try to guess whose card it is. If a player guesses correctly, he or she trades places with that person. If a player does not guess correctly, the player sits down.

5. Players should throw away the fact cards already used in the game. Then repeat steps 2 through 4 to play another round of the game.

6. For each round, standing players should place fact cards in the palms of players who have not yet had a turn in the game. Do this until all players have either had a turn to stand or receive a card.

Fact: ______________________

Fact: ______________________

Fact: ______________________

Fact: ______________________

Fact: ______________________

Fact: ______________________

Fact: ______________________

Fact: ______________________

Fact: ______________________

Fact: ______________________

Name _______________________

This Makes Me Happy

Make a poster that shows things that make you happy.

What You Need

- large poster board
- pictures of objects, people, food, animals, activities, and places that make you happy, or anything else that makes you happy
- markers
- scissors
- glue or tape
- materials to decorate the poster, such as glitter, dried cereal, colored tissue paper, stamps, foil, paint, yarn, beads, buttons, etc.

What You Do

1. Write the words **This Makes Me Happy** at the top of the poster. Then write your name somewhere on the poster.

2. Draw and tape or glue pictures onto the poster. Next to each picture, write to tell what the picture shows and why it makes you happy.

3. Decorate the poster.

4. Show your poster to your class or hang it up somewhere you will see it often to remind you of all the things that make you so happy!

Name ______________________

Same and Different Handprints

All people have differences and similarities. We all look kind of the same and kind of different. Compare your handprints with your classmates' handprints to see one way you are all the same and different.

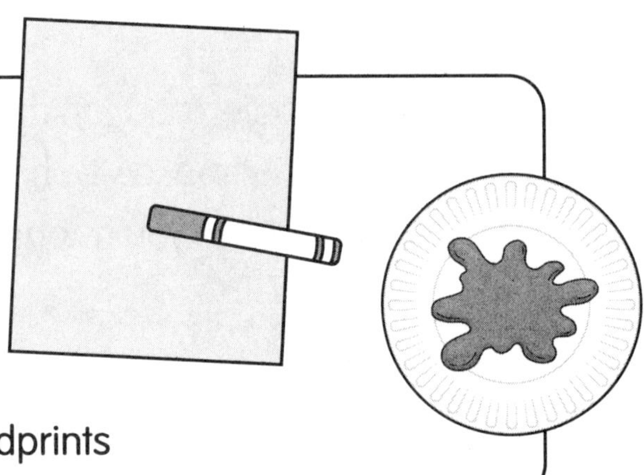

What You Need

- paints
- light-colored construction paper
- marker
- paper plate
- a place to hang or lay out all of the handprints

What You Do

1. Use the marker to write your name on the construction paper.

2. Pour paint onto the paper plate.

3. Dip each hand into the paint. Then press your hands onto the construction paper.

4. Let the paint dry. Then put your handprints with your classmates'.

5. Look at all of the handprints with your classmates and talk about how they are the same. Also talk about any differences you see.

   Culturally Responsive Lessons and Activities • EMC 8263 • © Evan-Moor Corporation

Name ________________________

Give Shout-outs!

A shout-out is something you say to tell someone thanks or that they did a good job.
Give shout-outs to the people in your family, and share the shout-outs with your class!

What You Need

- page 114
- colored construction paper
- scissors
- tape or glue
- crayons or markers

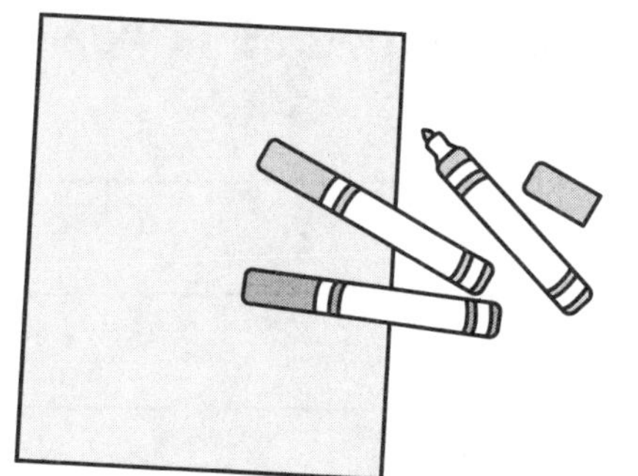

What You Do

1. Think of someone in your family whom you want to give a shout-out to.

2. Write inside each star on page 114 to tell whom each shout-out is for,
   and write what that person did to help you or make you happy.
   Or you can write something that the person did well.

3. Color the stars.

4. Cut out each star. Then tape or glue each one onto the construction paper.

5. Cut out each star again, leaving a border of the construction paper.

6. Share the shout-outs you made with your class.
   Tell the class why you love each person and why
   you are giving them a shout-out.

7. Take your shout-outs home or give each one
   to the person you made it for.

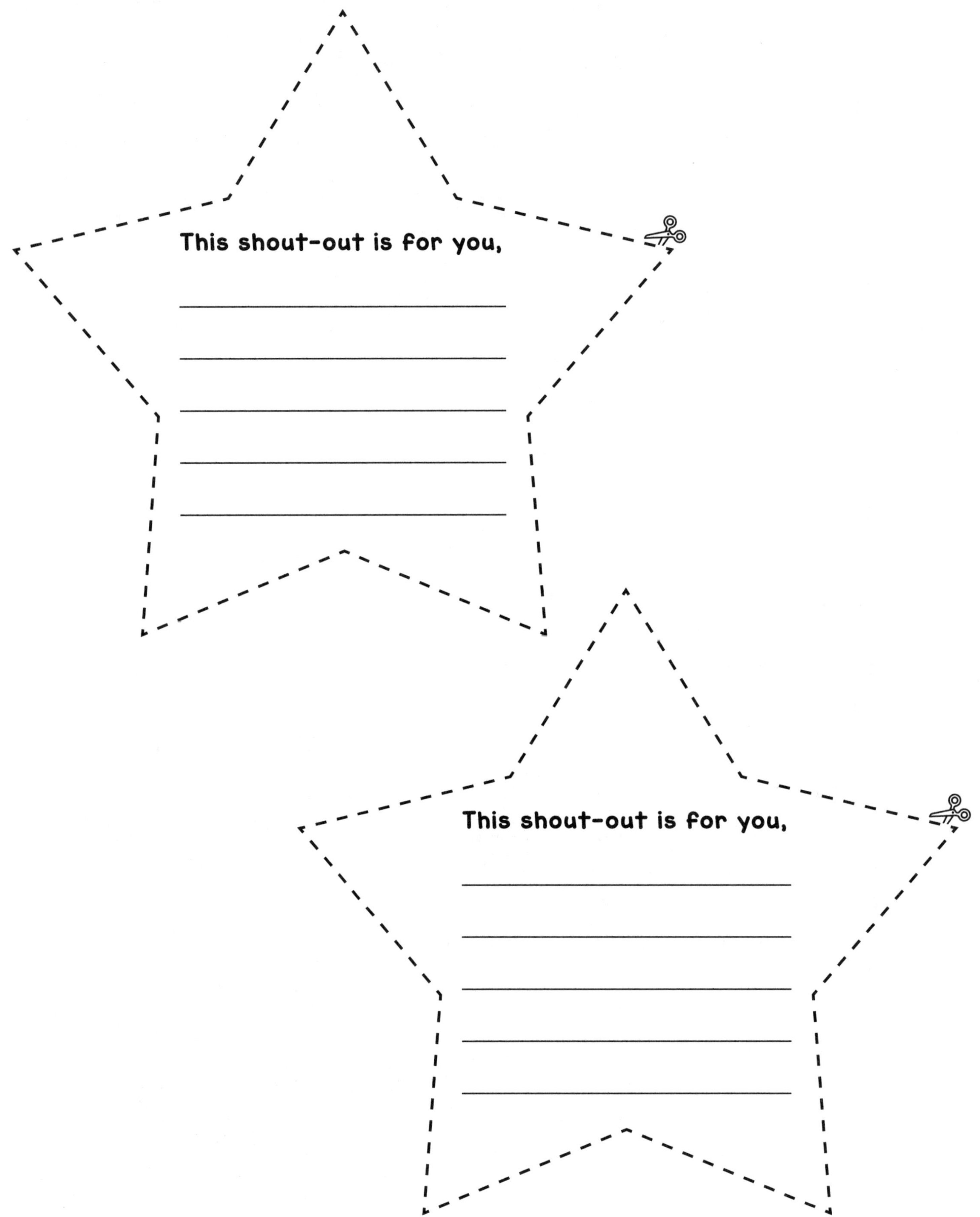
This shout-out is for you,

This shout-out is for you,

Name _______________________

Questions for Parent/Guardian

Every group of people has its own culture. Different families have their own cultures. Your culture includes the things you like to do, the foods you eat, the music you listen to, and much more! Take this page home, and ask an adult to write answers to the questions. Then bring this page back to your teacher.

1. What are some family traditions or activities that your family does together? Or are there any interests or hobbies that all of your family members enjoy?

   ____

   ____

2. What is something your child is proud of himself or herself about and likes to talk about?

   ____

   ____

3. Is there anything you have done as a family that is cultural in relation to ethnicity or nationality? Or are there any special events, holidays, or vacations you have done together as a family?

   ____

   ____

4. Is there anything else your child likes to talk about, such as an interest, an experience, or a fact about your family?

   ____

   ____

5. Are there any special foods or events your child looks forward to every week or every year?

   ____

Name ______________________

A Bit About Me, A Bit About You

Sit in a circle with your classmates. Write the names of all of your classmates.
The teacher will ask each student questions. When it is your turn to answer questions,
only you can talk. When it is another student's turn, listen carefully and then write one
thing you learned about that person next to his or her name.

Name	What I learned about this person

Name ___________________

Do You Agree?

Every person has his or her own opinions and beliefs. Sometimes we share beliefs with other people and sometimes we don't, and that is okay. Do this activity to tell what some of your beliefs are.

What You Need

- blown-up balloon

- markers

- a sentence that the teacher provides

- an area of the room to put all of the blown-up balloons where all students can reach them

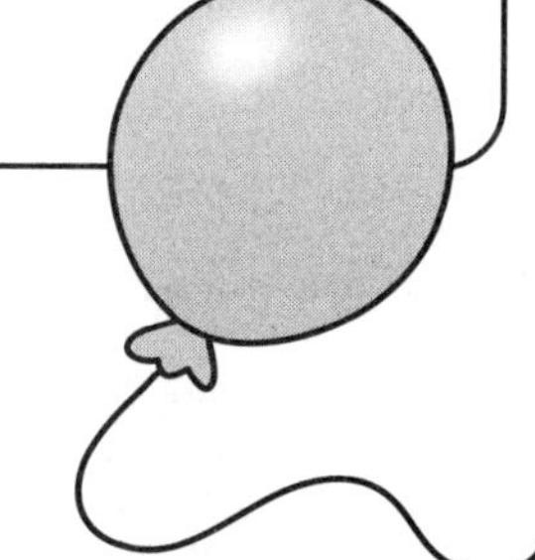

What You Do

1. Read the sentence that the teacher gives you. Then use a marker to write this sentence on your balloon.

2. If you agree with the sentence, write your name on the balloon. If you do NOT agree with the sentence, do not write your name.

3. Put your balloon in the area where all students are putting their balloons. The balloons will stay in this area.

4. Try to read as many balloons as you can. Read the sentences and read the students' names to see who agreed and who did not. Write your name on each balloon that you agree with.

5. When all students have finished reading and signing the balloons, talk with your classmates about the sentences you agreed with and the ones you didn't agree with.

Balloon Sentences

All people deserve to be treated with kindness and respect.

I can be friends with someone even if they have very different opinions from mine.

I feel more comfortable with people who look kind of like me, and I feel uncomfortable around people who look different.

I dislike people who have a different opinion from mine.

No matter what a person looks like, all people should be treated fairly.

I would rather have lots of gifts and things instead of friends.

I would like to have friends who look different from each other and who speak different languages.

I think all countries are just as good as each other.

I wish that nobody in the world would ever get hurt ever again.

Some people deserve to be treated badly.

You can tell how someone will act just by looking at that person.

All people deserve to have friends.

I love all people, no matter where they are from or what they look like.

Kindness and fairness are very important to me.

Food Is Part of Culture

This unit is about food and how it is an important part of every person's life experience. People need food to live. Yet we do not use food for survival only. We socialize with other people while we eat food. Many people eat certain foods only with their families. For some people it is a joy to eat daily meals with their loved ones. And food can be meaningful. Some people eat specific foods on specific occasions. Some people make or give food to others to show love. Some people like making foods with their friends and families. Food can help us remember times from the past and traditions. Every person's food preferences are different, but they are influenced by our cultures and our lives. Some people like trying many different kinds of foods, and some people do not. Keep in mind that food insecurity may be a very real problem for some of your students. Also, access to different kinds of foods differs for people based on geographic location and other factors. As you guide students through these topics, consider their varying world views as they share their experiences and make connections to their own lives.

The pages in this unit are reproducible. Reproduce the unit in its entirety or choose the pages that you wish to have your students do.

1. **Use Your Noodle! (pages 120 and 121)**
   Distribute one copy of each page to each student. Guide students in completing the pages independently.

2. **Have You Tried This Fruity Fruit? (pages 122 and 123)**
   Distribute one copy of each page to each student. Guide students in completing the pages independently. Then have students share their answers.

3. **Game Day Foods (page 124)**
   Distribute one copy of the page to each student. Guide students in completing the page independently. Then have students share their answers.

4. **New Year Celebration Foods (page 125)**
   Distribute one copy of the page to each student. Guide students in completing the page independently. Then have students share their answers.

5. **Make Your Perfect Celebration Plate (pages 126–128)**
   Distribute one copy of each page to each student. Guide students in completing the pages independently. Then have students share their answers.

6. **Twenty Questions Food Game (pages 129 and 130)**
   Distribute one copy of each page to each student. Provide students with the materials needed. Guide students in making and playing the game.

Name _______________________

Use Your Noodle!

Many people in different countries like to eat noodles. There are so many different ways to eat noodles! Look at the photos and read about the noodles below and on page 121. Color the circle under the kinds of noodles you have tried.

Italy – Ravioli

Pasta pockets filled with meat, cheese, or vegetables

Japan – Udon

Thick, chewy noodles that are often eaten in soup or with meat and vegetables

Fast Fact:

The country named for each noodle is not the only country where this food is eaten.

Argentina – Ñoquis

Dumplings (small lumps of dough), also known as gnocchi, which can be covered in sauce

Austria – Spaetzle

Small dumplings made with fresh eggs and often served with meat or gravy

Philippines – Pancit

Thin, long noodles cooked with spices, vegetables, and meat

Culturally Responsive Lessons and Activities • EMC 8263 • © Evan-Moor Corporation

Name _______________________

Use Your Noodle!, *continued*

Afghanistan – Ashak

Pasta dumplings filled with green onions and topped with tomato, mint, garlic, and plain yogurt

◯

Egypt – Koshary

Macaroni mixed with lentils, rice, tomatoes, onion, spices, oil, and vinegar

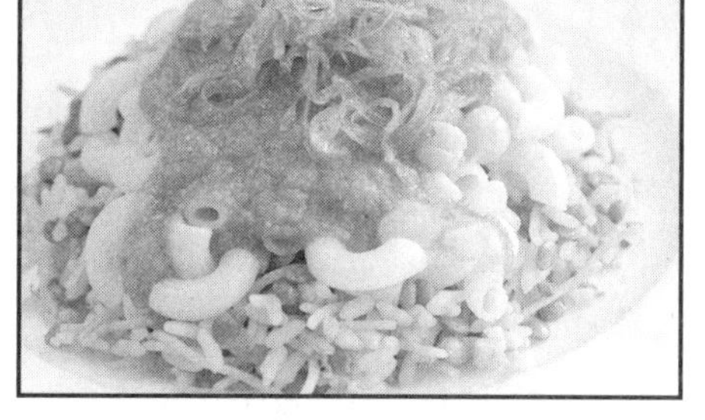

◯

Greece – Orzo

Short-cut pasta that looks like rice

◯

Morocco – Couscous

Tiny rolled-up balls of pasta that are so small they look like grain

◯

Thailand – Pad Thai

Thick, flat rice noodles that are cooked with spices, onions, and often meat, seafood, tofu, or vegetables

◯

China – Cellophane Noodles

Long noodles that are so clear they are also known as glass noodles, used in hot soups and stir-fries

◯

Name _______________________

Have You Tried This Fruity Fruit?

In some places, some fruits don't grow or can't be found easily. For example, some people eat pineapples almost every day because there are so many where they live. But some people have never even tried a pineapple!

Look at the photos and read the names of the fruits below and on page 123. Then fill in **yes** or **no** to tell if you have tried it before, or fill in **I would try it**.

coconut
- ○ yes
- ○ no
- ○ I would try it

watermelon
- ○ yes
- ○ no
- ○ I would try it

pomegranate
- ○ yes
- ○ no
- ○ I would try it

papaya
- ○ yes
- ○ no
- ○ I would try it

dragon fruit
- ○ yes
- ○ no
- ○ I would try it

persimmon
- ○ yes
- ○ no
- ○ I would try it

blueberry
- ○ yes
- ○ no
- ○ I would try it

cherry
- ○ yes
- ○ no
- ○ I would try it

nectarine
- ○ yes
- ○ no
- ○ I would try it

Name _______________________

Have You Tried This Fruity Fruit?, *continued*

custard apple

- ○ yes
- ○ no
- ○ I would try it

mango

- ○ yes
- ○ no
- ○ I would try it

passion fruit

- ○ yes
- ○ no
- ○ I would try it

breadfruit

- ○ yes
- ○ no
- ○ I would try it

raspberry

- ○ yes
- ○ no
- ○ I would try it

guava

- ○ yes
- ○ no
- ○ I would try it

kiwi

- ○ yes
- ○ no
- ○ I would try it

plum

- ○ yes
- ○ no
- ○ I would try it

star fruit

- ○ yes
- ○ no
- ○ I would try it

Name ___________________________

Game Day Foods

It's the day of the big rugby game. It's showing on TV around the world. Many families are watching the game together, and each family has its own favorite foods for game days. Read what each family eats and look at the photos. Color the face to show if you would want to eat those foods.

The Park family is watching the game from South Korea.
These are their favorite game day snacks:

crunchy dried squid

rice cakes in sauce

potato chips

The Farooqi family is from Pakistan, but they are in Britain watching the game.
These are their favorite game day snacks:

spiced chickpeas

meat pies

chips, or fries

The Garcia family is Mexican American. They are watching the game from the U.S.
These are their favorite game day snacks:

hot dogs

elote, or corn
with toppings

chicken wings

 Culturally Responsive Lessons and Activities • EMC 8263 • © Evan-Moor Corporation

Name _______________________

New Year Celebration Foods

Many different cultures celebrate the start of a new year. Different cultures or countries celebrate new year holidays at different times. For example, people in many countries celebrate New Year's Day on January 1 of each year. Many people in Iran and around the world celebrate Nowruz, the Iranian New Year, in March. People in many countries celebrate the Lunar New Year in February. Some people choose to celebrate the new year with special foods.

Look at the photos and read the sentences about the foods that each family makes to celebrate. Write a ✓ in the box to tell if you would want to eat what that family eats.

The Williams family makes a big seafood dinner.

The Lopez family always puts out cheeses to enjoy for the new year.

The Gupta family makes a huge pot of spicy stew to share.

The Ryan family always makes fried chicken and biscuits for the new year.

Name _______________________

Make Your Perfect Celebration Plate

Look at the photos below and on page 127. They show some foods that you may choose to eat for a special celebration. Cut out the foods that you would want to eat or try for the first time, and glue them onto the plate on page 128. On the lines, write why you chose each food. Last, compare your plate to your friends' plates!

Culturally Responsive Lessons and Activities • EMC 8263 • © Evan-Moor Corporation

bibimbap
tacos
salad
chow mein
ice cream
ramen
schnitzel
pancakes
pumpkin pie
chips and salsa
spaghetti
baklava
muffins
quiche
vegetables

Name ______________________

This is why I chose these foods:

____

____

____

____

____

Name _______________________

Twenty Questions Food Game

Make a game about food that you can play with your friends and family.
You can play with 2 or more people.

What You Need

- page 130
- scissors

What You Do

1. Cut out the cards on page 130.

2. Look at the photos on the cards and read about the foods. Keep in mind that each food is eaten in more than one country and not only the countries listed on the cards.

To Play

1. Place the cards facedown in a pile. Put the Master Foods List card where every player can see it.

2. When it is each person's turn, that person picks the top card and does not show it to anybody else.

3. The other player or players can ask 20 questions to try to guess what food the person has on his or her card. All of the questions must be yes-or-no questions.

Have Fun!

Master Foods List

Peri Peri Chicken	Poutine	Pho
Frikadeller	Paella	Moussaka
Amok Trey		

Peri Peri Chicken
South Africa, Portugal

Chicken cooked in a blend of spices, chiles, and flavors

Poutine   Canada

Potato fries topped with gravy and cheese curds

Pho   Vietnam

Soup filled with rice noodles and meat or vegetables, usually served with lime and mung bean sprouts

Frikadeller   Denmark

Mashed meat patties made of minced beef, milk, onions, and eggs

Paella   Spain

Rice cooked in a broth with tomatoes and vegetables or meat, sometimes spicy

Moussaka   Greece

Layers of eggplant and a cheesy sauce, sometimes also with potatoes or meat

Amok Trey   Cambodia

Fish coated in coconut milk and served in a banana leaf with vegetables

Class Book

This unit provides resources for you and your students to make a Class Book. The purpose of the book is for students to learn more about themselves and each other. It also helps you learn more about each of your students. As you introduce this project to students, keep in mind that some students may be happy to share details about themselves, and others may not feel comfortable doing so. It is important to create a safe space for students to share without feeling judged or uncomfortable about who they are and where they come from. This is intended to be an inclusive experience that creates positive relationships and fosters understanding of each other.

Getting Started

Reproduce the student pages for each student and allow them to complete the pages they wish to. Provide colored pencils, crayons, markers, decorative materials, scissors, and tape and glue for students. Each page students complete will be taped onto a sheet of colored construction paper.

1. **Our Class Book (page 133)**

   Distribute one copy of the page to each student. Have students read the text independently, or read the text aloud as they follow along silently.

2. **About Me (pages 134–136)**

   Distribute one copy of each page to each student. These questions are intended to guide students to reflect on themselves. Provide a quiet space for students to complete this activity. You may also wish to have them work on it at home. Explain that they can complete whatever items they wish to. Encourage students to make their pages colorful and unique by coloring and decorating them. Have them turn in their completed pages to you.

3. **My Family's Culture (pages 137–139)**

   Distribute one copy of each page to each student. Explain that not all of the activities may apply to every student, so they can choose to complete the activities that do apply. Encourage students to take these activities home to complete so they can share them with their families and get information from family members. Have students turn in their completed pages to you.

4. **My Name Page (pages 140–142)**

   Students will make a name page to start their section of the Class Book. There are three pages of alphabet letters. You may wish to provide many copies and have students share and use what they need. Students will color the letters of their name, cut them out, and glue them onto the sheet of construction paper you provide. Then they will write any special information they have about their name. Explain this part of the activity to students by asking them what they know about their name. Were they named after someone in their family? Does their name have a special meaning? If they do not know, encourage them to ask their family about it. Tell students to include any special information about their name on their name page. Have them turn in their completed pages to you.

5. **My Photo or Picture (page 143)**

   Distribute one copy of the page to each student. Explain to students that it is optional to include pictures of themselves in the class book. You may choose to take photographs of your students in the classroom and print them at school.

6. **My Dedication Page (page 144)**

   Distribute one copy of the page to each student. Explain to students that writing a dedication is optional.

7. **Creating the Class Book**

   (**What You Need**)

   - 1 sheet of construction paper for each activity page students complete

   - 2 pieces of poster board for the front and back covers

   - 3 loose leaf binder rings to hold the book together

   - 3-hole punch

   - tape

   (**What You Do**)

   - Give students the pages that they completed along with the corresponding number of sheets of construction paper. Have students tape each of their pages onto a sheet of construction paper and return them to you. Their My Name Page will already be on construction paper.

   - Gather all students' pages and either three-hole punch the pages yourself or have the students do it. Then use binder rings to assemble the pages into a book. Each student's name page will start that student's section of the book.

   - Use the poster board to create a front and a back cover for the book.

8. **Sharing the Class Book**

   There are many ways to approach sharing the Class Book. You know what will work best for your class. You may wish to consider the suggestions below:

   - Create a sign-up sheet for students to sign out the Class Book. Set aside a special time in class for that student to read the book. Give each student three days to look at it.

   - Allow each student to look at the book on a rotating schedule during reading time.

   - Draw craft sticks each week to see who gets to look at the book for the week. If the student finishes early, you can draw another craft stick and allow the next student to start their turn with the book.

   Culturally Responsive Lessons and Activities • EMC 8263 • © Evan-Moor Corporation

Name _______________

Our Class Book

Have you ever heard of a Class Book? It is a book that tells each person's story. Read the questions and answers about a Class Book.

Why is a Class Book important?

There are many students in your class. Some of them are your friends, and others you may not know as well. Think about if you walk into a room full of friends. How do you feel? Think about if you walk into a room full of people you don't know. How do you feel? Each person may feel differently.

When you make a Class Book, you get to know the people you are around every day. You learn things about them that you may have never known. You may understand them more. And when you understand them more, you may even become friends. A Class Book also helps your teacher get to know you better. You can show and tell things about yourself that you are proud of or that make you feel happy. You can also show and tell about things that are hard for you or that make you feel sad. When your teacher knows more about you, he or she can give you support when you need it.

How does a Class Book work?

Each student in your class completes pages for the book. You can complete the pages in any way you'd like to. You can be creative and show who you are through drawing pictures or writing. Some of the pages have activities that you complete with your family. After you finish the pages, you give them to your teacher. Then you and your classmates will work together in class to put together the Class Book. The book will be passed around and each student will have his or her own time to look through it. You will learn a lot about everyone and have a lot of fun reading the book!

Name ___________________________

About Me

Draw and write to tell about you.

What I like to do most:

5 things
that are important
to me are:

I am a
star at:

Name ____________________

About Me, *continued*

Draw and write to tell about you.

I wish I could:

This is my favorite place to be:

If I could change one thing, I would change:

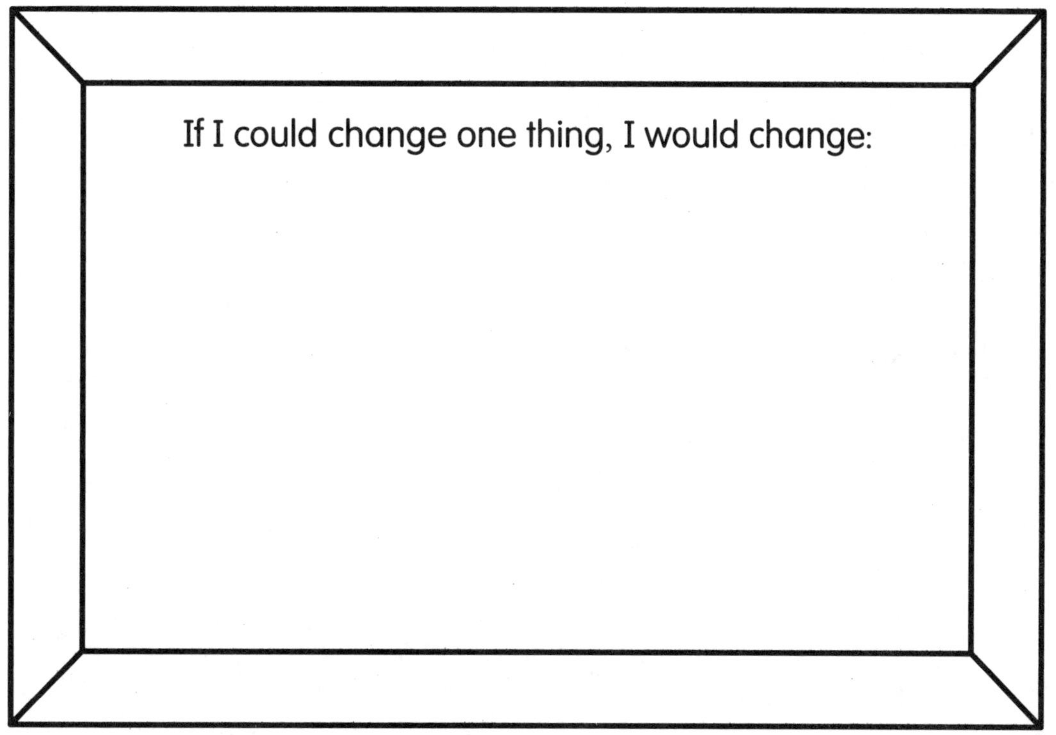

Name _______________________________

About Me, *continued*

Draw and write to tell about you.

Culturally Responsive Lessons and Activities • EMC 8263 • © Evan-Moor Corporation

Name ___________________________

My Family's Culture

Your family's culture is the traditions, habits, and values your family has. It's who you are as a family. Mark the box to show which things are part of your family's culture. Then write a few details about it. Write anything that is missing from the list in the last two boxes.

☐ holidays	
☐ celebrations	
☐ special foods	
☐ sports	
☐ religion	
☐ music, singing	
☐ exercise	
☐ community service	
☐ watching movies together	
☐ making things together	
☐	
☐	

Name _______________________________

My Family's Culture, *continued*

Do you have parents, grandparents, or family members who express their culture or cultures through the kinds of foods they make or the kinds of foods they eat? Talk to your family members and get the recipes from them. Write them on the recipe cards.

Recipe _______________________________

From the kitchen of _______________________________

Drawing of the food

Ingredients:

____

____

____

Directions:

____

____

____

Recipe _______________________________

From the kitchen of _______________________________

Drawing of the food

Ingredients:

____

____

____

Directions:

____

____

____

Name ___________________________

My Family's Culture, *continued*

Language is part of culture. Does your family speak a different language at home than what you usually speak at school? Write and draw to tell about it.

My family speaks this language: _______________________________

My family members come from these countries or places:

Cultural symbols can be flags, statues, colors, or a certain way of dressing.

A cultural symbol has meaning to the people from that culture.

Draw 2 cultural symbols below from your family's culture or cultures.

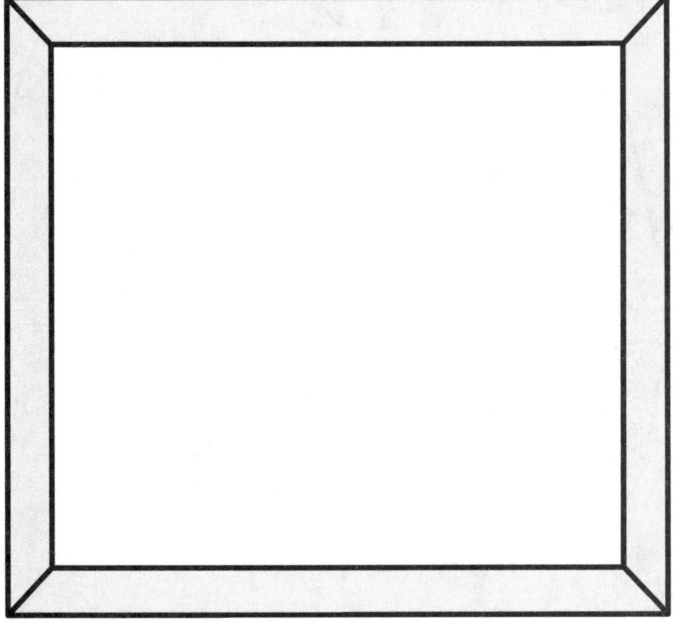
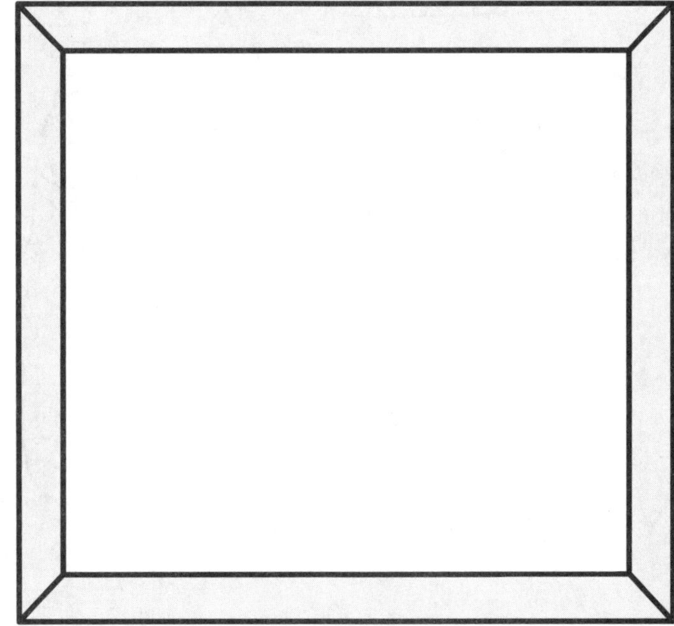

My Name Page

Color the letters of your name. Then cut them out and spell your name. Glue your name to a sheet of construction paper. Were you named after someone? Does your name have a special meaning? Write to tell about it below your name.

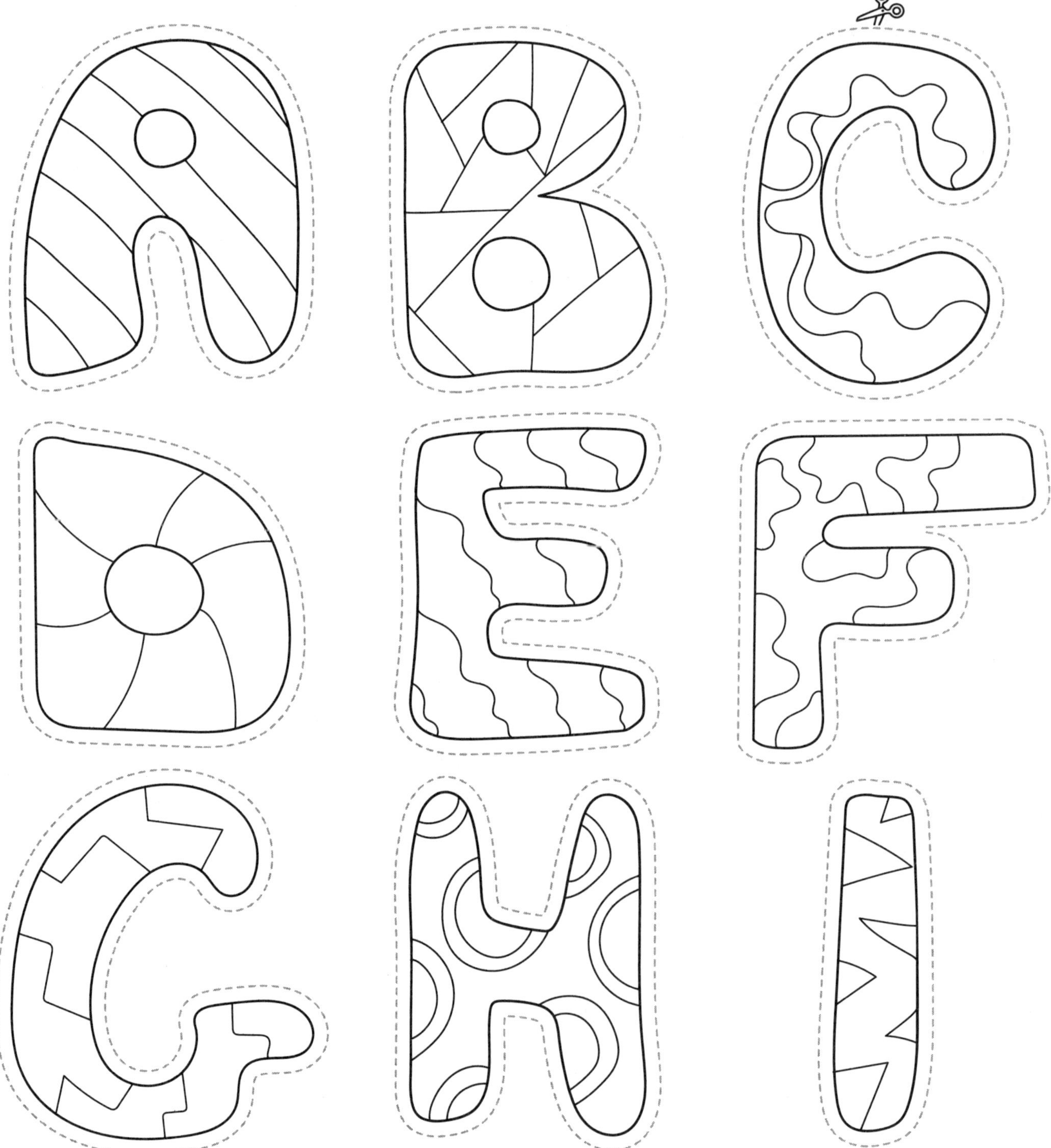

Culturally Responsive Lessons and Activities • EMC 8263 • © Evan-Moor Corporation

My Name Page, *continued*

Color the letters of your name. Then cut them out and spell your name. Glue your name to a sheet of construction paper. Were you named after someone? Does your name have a special meaning? Write to tell about it below your name.

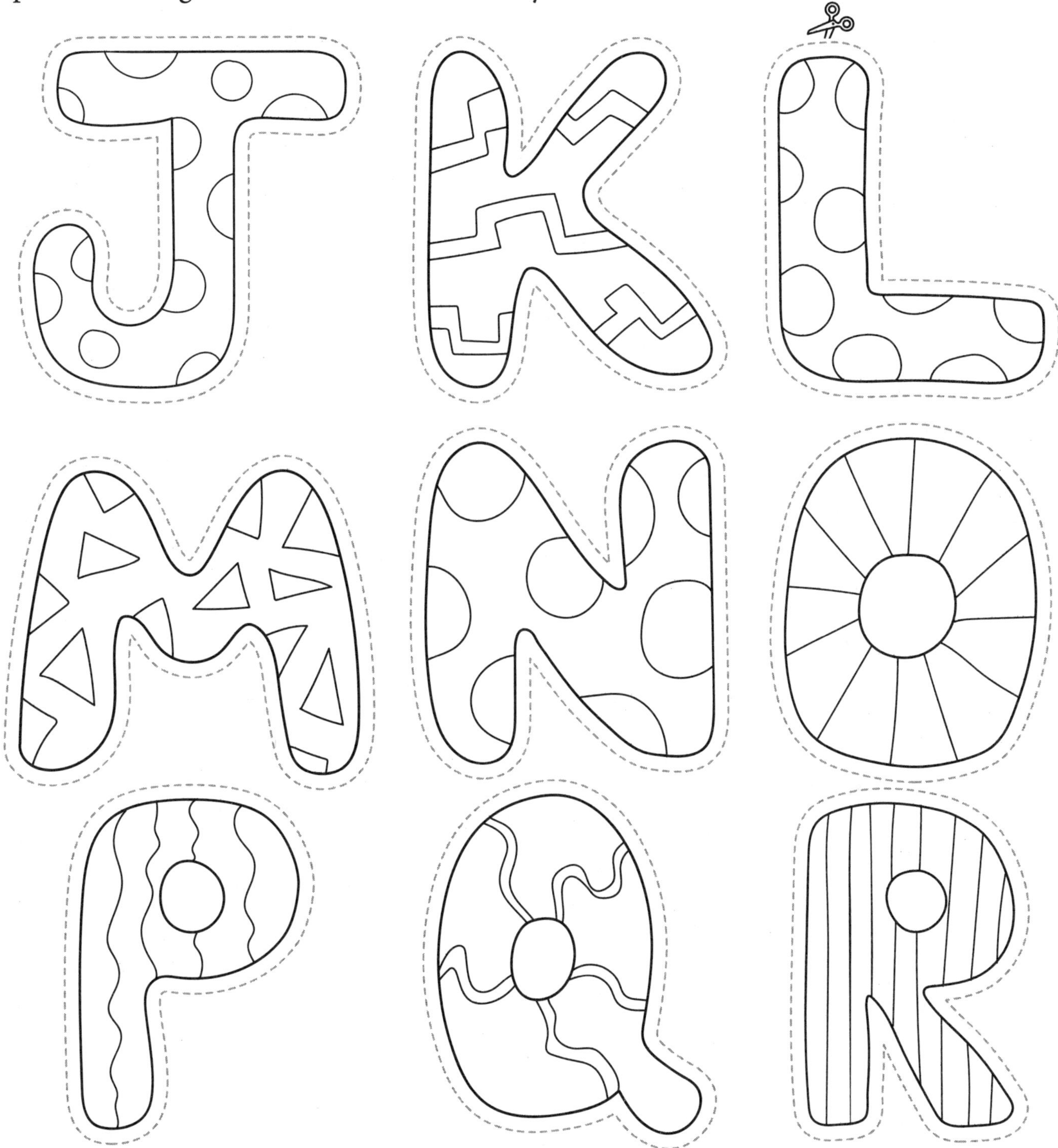

My Name Page, *continued*

Color the letters of your name. Then cut them out and spell your name. Glue your name to a sheet of construction paper. Were you named after someone? Does your name have a special meaning? Write to tell about it below your name.

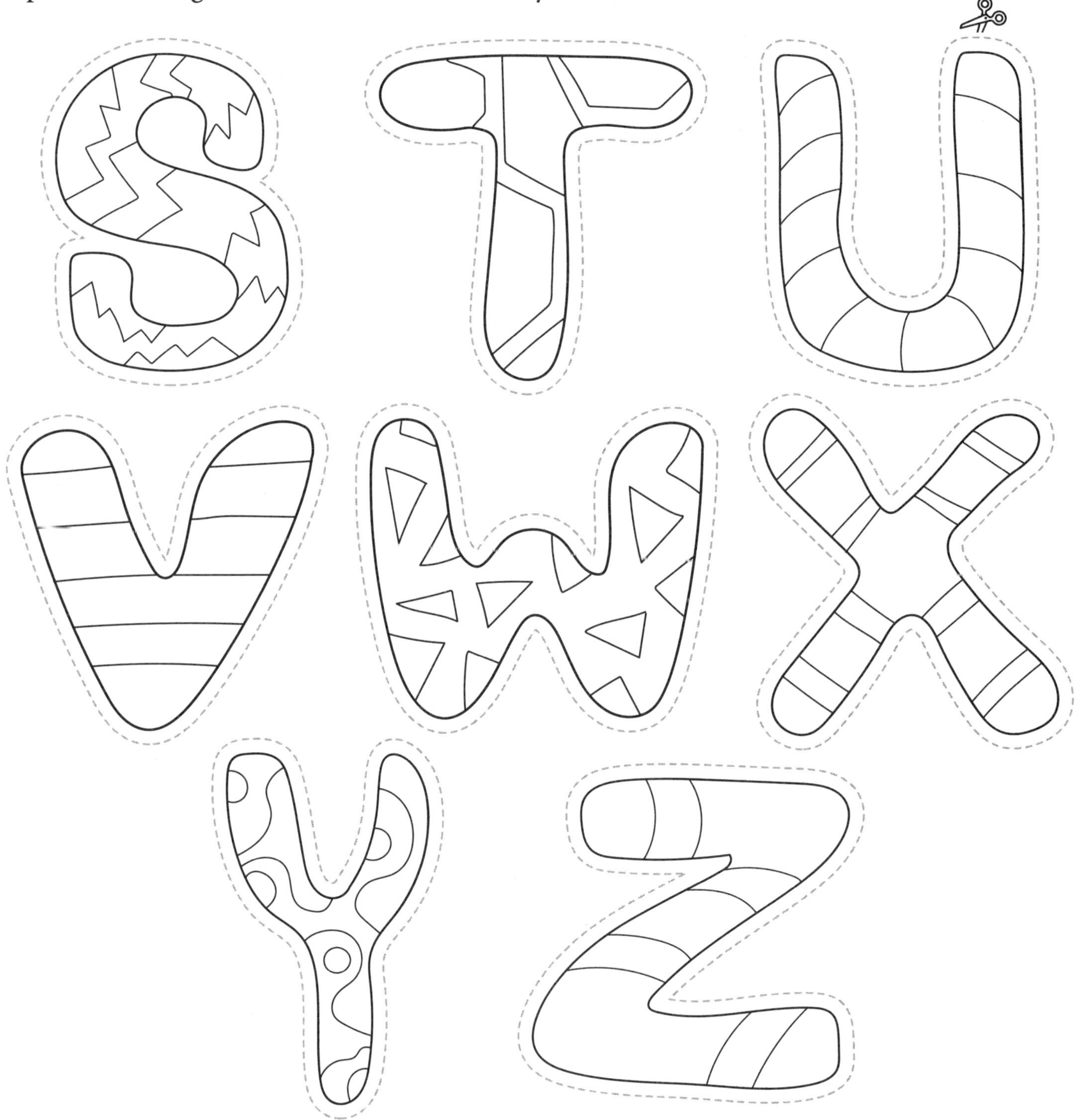

Culturally Responsive Lessons and Activities • EMC 8263 • © Evan-Moor Corporation

Name _______________________

My Photo or Picture

Ask someone to take a photo of you and help you print it. Then tape it in the square below. Or you can draw a picture of yourself in the square. Last, draw on and decorate the frame around the square.

Name ___________________________

My Dedication Page

You wrote pages for a class book. A lot of book authors write a dedication. A dedication page tells who the author wants to thank or show appreciation to. You can dedicate your book pages to people you care about or admire. You can dedicate your book pages to one person or multiple people.

Draw and write to tell whom you want to dedicate your book pages to.

Culturally Responsive Lessons and Activities • EMC 8263 • © Evan-Moor Corporation